The Castle
Ground

THE ANATOMY OF SUBURBIA

J. M. RICHARDS

ILLUSTRATED BY
John Piper

faber and faber

This edition first published in 2011
by Faber and Faber Ltd
Bloomsbury House, 74–77 Great Russell Street
London WC1B 3DA

Printed and bound by CPI Group (UK) Ltd, Croydon, CR0 4YY

A CIP record for this book is available from the British Library

ISBN 978–0–571–28159–6

Contents

v

The more things change . . .

This book is not really about the suburbs but about participation. It has recently come to be recognized that territorial planning, which means the long-term shaping of the setting of people's lives —the shaping of the *environment,* as it is fashionable to call it—ought not to consist simply of those in authority taking decisions to which everyone else is expected to conform. We now see planning as a process, not an edict, and a process in which all—the planners and the planned-for—must take part if it is to be successful.

It is thus that another fashionable word has come into use: participation. Genuine public participation in the planning process demands three things: that the planners should work to a brief based on a detailed study of people's wants and needs; that the public as a whole should consent to the plans made; that there is allowance for the direct involvement of the public in creating the ultimate environment for which the plan is only a framework— and a provisional framework at that.

The last of these requirements is perhaps the most important, and certainly the most difficult, to achieve. Hitherto a plan has too often been regarded as an end-product, a mechanism for making decisions which then have only to be implemented; whereas it is not the end of a process but the beginning. It is during the course of implementing a plan that its value is assessed, its validity established, its details—or, if necessary, its actual structure—amended as new needs and opportunities reveal themselves. An environment only matures when the people inhabiting it have visibly influenced it by the way they have used it.

It was in this long-term sense that *The Castles on the Ground* was written in the 1940s; and that perhaps is the best justification for republishing it. One of the book's aims was to explain how the suburb, as it had developed in England during the couple of generations preceding 1939, had grown to be the prime example of a style of environment largely created by its inhabitants. It is not the only example; any man-made environment answers to this description up to a point. The most pertinent criticism of the recent attempts to replan city centres like Piccadilly Circus and Covent Garden is that the human value of such centres derives from the kind of life that has been lived in them over the years, a life that would be exterminated by total rebuilding, especially in the form of a finite architectural design which leaves no room for contributions by ordinary people.

The problem is that the cherished character of such places is predominantly accidental, and the most difficult thing in architecture is to design a happy accident. Yet the suburban scene described in *The Castles on the Ground* is an accumulation of happy accidents. Architects (or, more likely, builders' draughtsmen) may have designed the houses. The local surveyor, or an estate developer, may have laid out the roads. The occupants may have added planting and other outdoor embellishments. But no one person has made a total design. No-one from outside has imposed his own vision so as to dictate the ultimate form.

In this sense the suburb is different in kind from the town or city, and another of the book's aims was to show that the suburb is neither the town spread thin nor the country built close, but a quite different type of development with its own inimitable characteristics. Its physical nature and its aesthetic qualities are almost wholly the product of the people living there—the product, in fact, of participation, though the term was not yet in use in 1946 when the book was published.

The Castles on the Ground also attempted to establish architectural criticism as criticism of the *results* of building, not of buildings as such; a direction in which today's emphasis on the environment also leads. That was a thesis it was natural to put forward in relation to a place where the whole was obviously greater —and more to be admired—than the parts. The multifarious components of the suburban scene could not be looked at separately or the scene itself would disappear. And the fact that the quality of the environment was not, in the suburb, dependent on the quality as architecture of the individual buildings relates to our recent discovery that buildings designed by good architects do not always enhance the environment, and that poorly designed buildings can sometimes, by accident, do exactly that.

But besides having lessons to teach the modern environmentalist, the suburb has its own intrinsic importance as the physical expression of a way of life that may at first have had only peripheral significance but, as a consequence of greater mobility, is increasingly becoming the way of life of the typical Englishman. With the social decay and the gradual depopulation of city centres, the power base of the nation and the source of its attitudes and opinions is moving daily away from the cities; not always into suburbs, but into places owing at least partial allegiance to the suburban way of life.

Changes have of course taken place in the suburbs since *The Castles on the Ground* was written, so much so that the suburb depicted there may strike the present reader as being no more than a period piece. But the most obvious changes are only superficial. One is the progressive intensification of its original characteristics resulting from the mere passage of time. The leafy suburbs I described in 1946 are now leafier still, and their expanse of roofs is masked by taller trees—except of course where a new main road has opened a way through, an innovation that is necessary here and there but one that directly contradicts the closed-in, self-contained style which is the essence of suburbia. A place where this has happened must be accounted just one casualty in the unending war between the established order and the pressure of new forces. We must expect this war to be partly fought over suburban territory because suburban life and the people who create it exist perpetually on the fringe of change; they are a sensitive barometer and gauge of the rise and decline of social habits, of which motoring is one, and values and aspirations.

The many other superficial changes in the suburban scene since 1946 become evident the moment one goes back there: the baker's boy, with whose daily call *The Castles on the Ground* begins, no longer halts his elegantly panelled pushcart under the shade of the laburnums; the peace of Sunday afternoon in the garden is disturbed by the hum and clatter of a dish-washer heard through the kitchen window; the garden itself is perhaps less industriously tended as a result of the rival attractions of package holidays abroad; the gravestones in the churchyard have been uprooted and ranged tidily along one of the walls so that a motor-mower can cut the grass smoothly, which the new young vicar prefers; the parade of privately owned shops has given way to a vast supermarket, and one of the problems it and its customers have to contend with is indicated by the double yellow line that follows the curve of its pavement.

This yellow line is significant because it identifies a far more fundamental change. Those just described are only changes of fashion; they reflect improvements in technology or fluctuations in the economy. But the intrusion of the motor-car into the suburb does more than imperil the peace and seclusion so highly valued there; the motor-car, as a new and disruptive element, is common to all environments, and so the distinctive nature of the suburban one is compromised by its presence.

It would be a mistake, nevertheless, to regard the motor-car as wholly alien to the suburban ethos. The suburb is not an archaic place concerned only with the escape it offers from the disquieting phenomena of the modern world. Though the motor-car is undoubtedly one of these phenomena, at the same time it belongs to the very culture that gave rise to the suburb itself and which makes it distinct in kind from the city and the country—see Chapter 6. The suburb may still have to adjust itself in many ways to the car-owning habit, but the motor-car has already been captured and tamed by it. The motor-car becomes a creature of the suburb especially at week-ends; besides providing the family with a self-contained capsule for excursions into the world beyond, allowing it to preserve its separate identity however far it travels—a capsule orbiting in alien space but programmed to splash down again by supper-time—the motor-car also provides an extra focus of activity within the suburban homeland. Sunday morning can be spent, the whole family helping, washing or tinkering with the family car, an activity wholly in accordance with the suburban way of life before the motor-car entered it.

Compactness, I declared in 1946, is all; and the seclusion and integrity of the traditional suburb are not endangered by the presence of the motor-car so much as by the planning concepts and controls that arrived with the motoring age. The rapid spread of out-of-town building, the growth of motorized shopping, and more especially the proliferation of car-dependent housing estates, have further confused the picture that used to be so clear: a picture of each culture—urban, rural and suburban—enjoying the distinct environment that had been evolved to suit it.

As a result of these new planning controls, the growth of the modern suburb is less spontaneous than it used to be when a suburban community simply crystallized round some nuclear point like an old village green or a new railway station, was then fostered by enterprising builders anticipating a demand and slowly became self-contained through the accretion of shops and schools and tennis-clubs and choral societies and cottage-hospitals—again in response to a demand—until its separate identity was duly recognized for local government purposes.

This process has now been speeded up and, more important, has become a planned process. In our day the concept of territorial and land-use planning has been accepted as a necessity, in town, country and suburb, because of the disasters resulting from unplanned development on an increasing scale and because of the growing pressure on land. It now plays an essential part in the machinery of government in spite of being relatively an innovation. The key piece of legislation, the 1947 Town and Country Planning Act, came along a year after the publication of *The Castles on the Ground*, which explains perhaps why the suburbs the book describes seem to have receded so far into the past. This explains, too, why it was necessary to make it clear in the book that only the mature, fully developed specimens of suburbia were being described and that there existed also numerous so-called suburbs—the result of unplanned development—wholly lacking the environmental qualities of the true suburb: a mere scattering of buildings around the edges of towns.

Planning controls have at least brought some order into this proliferation of random building; sometimes tentatively, sometimes vigorously, according to the ability of the officials administering them. Moreover the influence of professionally trained planners has introduced into the suburb devices like Radburn-type layouts based on footpath access, which have done something to offset the disruptive effect of the motor-car. Architecturally, nevertheless, the conscious aim is now unity instead of variety. Because of their extent, and the professional expertise that has been lavished on them, the housing schemes of the small minority of enlightened developers and the residential neighbourhoods of the new towns display this unity of architectural form and layout most prominently. The new towns have, by their example, transformed English housing outside the big cities almost as drastically in the last twenty years as tall blocks of flats have transformed it inside. But a new town cannot be equated with the essential suburb I have been describing, for the obvious reason that it is designed for working as well as living; it has factories as well as houses; it aspires to being what is called a balanced community, which may have its advantages but not the particular advantage of providing an environment tailored exclusively to the residential needs of suburban man.

The new town and its forerunner the garden city create, by definition, an instant environment, designed by architects and managements to be complete as soon as built, functionally and visually. There is little scope for do-it-yourself activities on the part of the inhabitants, enabling them to achieve a sense of unity, because unity of a different kind has already been imposed from outside. Perhaps we can attribute to this some of the failings of the new towns. It is acknowledged that they lack social coherence, and that this is partly the fault of their diffuse layouts which discourage neighbourliness—a virtue, incidentally, characteristic of the slums from which many of the new towns' first inhabitants came, but one that the suspicious and introverted English find surprisingly difficult to recover once contact, as it were, has been lost. (Is there any significance in the fact that what we call a semi-detached house the Americans call a semi-attached?) But the lack of coherence in the new towns is surely just as much the fault of a passive acceptance of the new environment induced in the inhabitants by the apparent finality of the design.

The price we have had to pay for the undoubted benefit that planned development has brought to the community as a whole is, therefore, less neighbourliness of a spontaneous kind. There is a reasonable amount of community life in the new towns in the shape of societies and clubs with flourishing memberships—perhaps more than in the old-style suburb—but these social facilities, and the rituals they engender, must be allowed to strike physical roots so as to create an environment that satisfies the user because he has helped to shape and modify it at every stage.

The next need therefore is to discover how to use our enlightened planning legislation, and the new techniques of research that enable us to base building programmes on a true analysis of people's needs, to foster designs that are flexible and adaptable enough to encourage user-participation as well as the exploitation of all kinds of happy accident.

The architectural ritual of the older suburbs was inseparable from their social ritual. The two developed simultaneously. As life includes more uncertainties, as government becomes more impersonal and communities more unstable, the need for such a ritual—and the need to identify ourselves, through the pattern into which we ourselves have moulded it, with the one place we regularly return to—grows greater. In the absence of a ritual there is only a vacuum.

The new suburbs, though presumably nourishing the embryos of the self-contained, elaborately endowed communities of the next generation, are not yet easy to distinguish amidst the random developments on the edges of towns that the motoring age has promoted. They have not yet acquired form or identity, not usually being based, like the older suburbs, on existing villages absorbed into the outskirts of the spreading city; so that it is difficult to tell with most of them where they begin, and while we are still looking for the centre we find ourselves coming out on the other side. This is partly because today's suburb has an uncomfortably high proportion of open space—not space put to a good use like the secluded public garden in the old suburb, where children sailed boats and their older sisters helped them feed the swans, but wasteful space required only by the planning regulations: games fields round all the schools even though the pupils could easily be transported to less expensive fields outside the built-up area; roads made unnecessarily wide to conform with the council engineer's rule-book; broad green verges on either side of them which are only there to make the engineer's service-pipes easier to get at.

Once inside the new suburb we may be tempted to criticise further, and point to the dismal failure of most speculative builders' housing to achieve better standards of design in spite of the recent improvement in the design of manufactured goods, including domestic equipment and furniture. We may complain that prefabricated houses, even when conscientiously designed, give a disappointingly brittle look to parts of the suburb, that picture-windows punch unexpected holes in bungalow walls and that the garages now provided for every home make gaps in the once continuous line of fence and hedge, thus adding to the impression of excessive openness; and we may assert that there is very little evidence of participation. The lines of washing which, in crowded cities, promptly humanise the most barren housing schemes are of course unthinkable here; or, rather, are kept out

of sight in the back garden, and are decreasingly to be found even there because there's now a launderette in the shopping piazza. But we must not be deceived; time and the growth of vegetation will work wonders. Some of the old suburbs whose scenic richness and complexity we admire today must have looked, when first built, very like the new estates we find so featureless and bleak.

The qualities, moreover, that we were so ready to appreciate in 1946 were not even at that time the qualities sought after when the suburbs we value because of them were built. The builder's vernacular of their day was all they started with in the way of an architectural vocabulary, and this was no more than the raw material out of which something different and peculiarly its own gradually evolved. By the time another suburban style has, as a result of a similar process, not only matured in its turn but been identified and recorded and analysed by the sophisticated, we can be sure that it will have ceased to respond to changed suburban needs.

The problem, if the same creative process is to continue, is that the present-day planned suburb not only imposes, unlike its predecessor, a regular and inflexible pattern, but also an architect's sophisticated taste. His taste is alien, not because there is anything fundamentally wrong with the modern architectural idiom but because, in the suburbs, architecture is not the criterion by which taste is governed—in the most successful suburbs it is not governed at all. The elements of which their scenery is composed are not, as the following pages take pains to demonstrate, looked at as examples of design, good or bad; who chooses a residential suburb for its architecture? Its houses and trees and lampposts and hedgerows are all one, and the critic who appraises them in terms of conventional design standards misconceives the indivisible nature of the suburban vernacular.

In this self-conscious age the kind of environment suburban man is seeking will not grow as spontaneously as it used to do; only by someone taking thought. That is the normal role of the architect, but if architects are going to have any part in designing the new suburbs they will have to exchange their customary arrogance for a becoming humility. The suburbs are no place for monuments to their initial builders, whose part is minimal. We must not expect people to settle down contentedly, and immediately to find fulfil-ment, in an environment designed from outside and on the basis of someone else's idea of what they ought to be given. If we exclude public participation from the environment-building process we shall find that, instead of offering suburban man the refuge he has enjoyed in the past, we are offering him something like a prison; instead of an outlet for his creative instincts, a place which compels him to believe that creation is not for him, where there are even rules about the colour he may paint his front door.

J. M. RICHARDS
1973

The Castles on the Ground

1

The Englishman's Home

Ewbank'd inside and Atco'd out, the English suburban residence and the garden which is an integral part of it stand trim and lovingly cared for in the mild sunshine. Everything is in its place. The abruptness, the barbarities of the world are far away. There is not much sound, except perhaps the musical whirr and clack of a mowing machine being pushed back and forth over a neighbouring lawn and the clink of cups and saucers and a soft footfall as tea is got ready indoors. There is not much movement either: a wire-haired terrier lazily trotting round the garden in a not very hopeful search for something new to smell, and the pages of a newspaper being turned and refolded by some leisurely individual in a deck chair. It is an almost windless day. The leaves of the virginia creeper (*ampelopsis veitchii*) which climbs the rough-cast wall just behind the window of the best bedroom hardly stir, and even the birds only hop—and flutter a few feet in the air, and hop again—along the ornamental ridge of the red-tiled roof.

Perhaps a tradesman's van is making its rounds. Perhaps at this moment, on the other side of the screen of privet hedge and may and laburnum which separates the garden scent of new grass cuttings from the warm peppery scent that radiates from asphalt pavements in summertime, the baker's boy is halting his cart. In another moment he will push open the low wooden gate with its embossed copper name-plate on the rail, and will carelessly let it swing to behind him as he strides up the gravel path with his basket of loaves on his arm. But this is only the tradesman's entrance, and the faint squeak of the hinge and the sound the latch makes as the gate swings back will not be very disturbing; nor will his footsteps as he passes behind the green-painted trellis with the rockery at its foot towards the kitchen door at the side of the house.

Inside it is more peaceful still. The sunlight coming through the bottle glass of the front door falls in irregular blotches on the coconut mat made by blind ex-service men, on the fumed oak hatstand and on the wall-rack holding a variety of walking sticks collected on summer holidays, including one with a spiked ferrule and a sprig of edelweiss cut in the wood below the handle. These blotches of sunlight make the narrow hall seem rather dark by contrast. It smells faintly of furniture polish and somewhat more faintly of the American cloth of which the hood of a folding perambulator is made, a perambulator for which there is really not enough room in the hall, as the visitor will soon discover if he steps too confidently past the foot of the stairs. The far part of the hall is lighter because a door is slightly ajar, and through it there is a glimpse of the drawing room: a sofa with loose covers in flowered chintz, faded with much laundering, cream paint, the corner of a piano with framed photographs on it and a bay window with leaded panes, the centre part opening to the ground and leading down a couple of steps to the bright garden.

We could explore further, but perhaps this is enough to show that the house we have been looking at is simply the ordinary Englishman's home. The picture we have been painting is the picture the ordinary Englishman has in his mind when he is away at the war, or travelling about on business or living in digs in the middle of town till such time as he can afford a home of his own. It is rather an idyllic picture, but then the Englishman, being an optimist, thinks idyllically. For different Englishmen, of course, the picture varies in detail—but not very much. We have described the day-dream of the Englishman who belongs to one of the more prosperous suburbs—Cheam, perhaps, or Rickmansworth or Mill Hill—and to the class that wears a linen collar to go to work in, but we could just as easily have chosen an Englishman a little lower in the social scale and described his ideal villa instead, set but a short way back from the bustle of some arterial road in

Osterley or the outskirts of Birmingham. This one has but a modest lawn in front, perhaps with a cast stone bird-bath, and a wooden paling instead of a hedge of luxuriant flowering shrubs and trees; but this, it should be said, is chiefly because it is so much newer. There may only be a number on the gate, on a small oval china plate, instead of a name. Instead of the pillared or half-timbered porch there is a simpler brick arch beneath a plain tiled gable, and instead of the rack full of walking sticks in the hall a china umbrella stand.

Alternatively we could have looked a little higher in the social scale and set the house in its own grounds at the centre of a circular gravel drive bordered with rhododendrons and variegated laurel and other shrubs. We would then have mentioned the scent of Surrey pines and the fact that the front hall contains a polished table with a china bowl on it full of visiting cards. Beyond this hall we would have noted a larger lounge hall with oak-panelled walls instead of wallpaper or lincrusta, and at the end of it an open-well staircase with polished treads, lighted by its own round-topped window. This, as in the other houses, is leaded into rectangular panes, but it has a stout oak transom and a small inset of coloured heraldic glass. In the hall, in addition to the faint smell of furniture polish we would have noted an even fainter scent of Pears' soap coming from the downstairs cloakroom.

But in essence the picture remains the same. It is each individual Englishman's idea of his own home, except for the cosmopolitan rich, a minority of freaks and intellectuals and the very poor— and even for the latter it is what they would dream about if anyone could dream about what they have never known and if the fight for existence allowed time for much dreaming.

On the other hand, this is also a picture of the suburban villa itself. Besides representing the home idealized by the individual, it also represents an architectural type, and as such is the despair of people of taste. Whenever the present state of English architecture is discussed, whenever contemporary standards of design are analysed—only to be condemned—the suburb is named as the villain of the piece. Is it not, exclaim its critics, at the same time the prime example of the debasement of modern taste, and the spiritual home of the sentiments—or sentimentalities—on which this taste is nourished?

We well know the epithets used to revile the modern suburb—'Jerrybethan', and the rest—and the scornful finger that gets pointed at spec-builder's Tudor with its half-inch boards nailed flat to the wall in imitation of oak timbering, though perhaps we should not criticize so fiercely the architectural idiom the suburb has adopted as its own if we understood the instincts and ideals it aims to satisfy, and how well, judged by its own standards, it often succeeds in doing so. But to begin with the idiom itself. It is a thoroughly familiar one, not difficult to define in a few words. In its earlier days—that is, towards the end of last century—the suburban villa had a slate roof more often than a tiled one, but with a crest of ornamental tiles along the ridge. It had rather steep gables with perforated barge-boards painted dark green, sash windows, also painted dark green, and walls (when not hidden by ivy) either of a greyish rough-cast or of red and yellow bricks arranged in patterns. It had a small round window in the point of the gable, and a rather clumsy dark green porch with sides panelled in obscured glass of different colours, standing on a flight of cement steps.

A generation later—say by the end of King Edward VII's reign—it has become less upright in shape and more cheerful in colour. It was now a beefy red, red tiled roofs with dormer windows, and walls partly of red brick and partly hung with tiles. But this general redness was relieved by plenty of white-painted woodwork, especially in the shape of balconies and bay windows with close set balustrades and corner posts, turned and chamfered. Thick bars, also painted white, subdivided the windows into rectangular panes, for plate glass had now gone out of fashion. The high gabled porch had been replaced by a sort of lean-to verandah with a red tiled floor, and the ivy by a daintier creeper.

Later still, in the 'twenties and 'thirties, the redness remained—

at least in the roof and chimney stacks—but the white paint had given place to natural-coloured oak; oak beams criss-crossed the large gable that, with one slope extending almost to the ground, formed the front of the house; the porch, shaped like half a lych-gate, was of oak, and so were the frames and sills of the windows. The windows themselves were of metal, leaded into square or diamond panes. Crazy paving in the front garden had replaced the gravel path and, indoors, rustic brick fireplaces had replaced the black-leaded grates and painted mantel-pieces.

Such are some of the superficial differences between the sub-urban villas of three generations, but their similarities are much more significant than their differences. Old and new, we can take them all as one; for as well as being the same in essence for the city man, for his clerk and for the man who delivers the clerk's groceries, the suburban villa's sameness extends back in time to the day when the city man's father set up in married life at Bedford Park in 1882. The suburban style—that style which is, we are told, the very citadel of debased and vulgar taste—is, in fact, part of the background of the England we have all grown up in.

There is the puzzle which it is the purpose of this book to try to elucidate. On the one hand, we have the alleged deficiencies of suburban taste; on the other we have the appeal it holds for ninety out of a hundred Englishmen, an appeal which cannot be explained away as some strange instance of mass aberration. It is a puzzle of which we are specially conscious today, when we see the spread of suburbia about us, and are uneasily aware that the most recent of the three specimens of the suburban villa just described—the suburban villa of our own generation—seems to exist in its own right without being particularly concerned with the standards of good taste and bad taste by which we are generally taught that such things should be judged. Yet there is no doubt about the appeal and even the charm of the suburban environment. These are not only embodied in the kind of nostalgic reminiscence with which this book began, and which on analysis might turn out to be but an accidental by-product of suburbia itself. They are also embodied in the preference on the part of practical people for an environment possessing certain attributes, which they recognise instinctively even though they leave them undefined. The suburban environment is the choice of people who know what they like, and the architecture of the suburb may even be called a true contemporary vernacular.

Now the absence of a contemporary vernacular style is the one thing that all the critics of architecture agree in deploring. They see the history of English architecture stretching back to a golden age when it was harmoniously attuned to the needs and aspirations of the community it served. In those times—that is, until about a century and a half ago—there was but one way in which people built, but one style, which had evolved gradually and which was not the product of conscious choice. Then architecture, for reasons we need not go into here, disintegrated, and there followed an age of eclecticism. What we all see now is the need for a new universal idiom to replace the present bewildering multiplicity of applied styles, an idiom that shall be natural to our time and as capable of unselfconsciously adapting itself to our own needs and aspirations as the Georgian vernacular did to those of the eighteenth century; something more than a new set of architectural mannerisms; something based on a newly found public ability to think and feel architecturally.

Such an idiom, it is said, cannot be manufactured. It has to grow, with its roots in the instincts and basic structure of the society that adopts it. Yet those who are aware of the need for a new architectural idiom, too often envisage either one recreated from the past—as William Morris did—or one contrived synthetically to meet a coming world half-way. The former is dead beyond revival; the latter is powerless to be born until it can have breathed into it the animating spirit of popular sanction.

This implies no denial of the authenticity of the new architectural pattern that this century has already shown signs of producing—the so-called modern architecture, based on geometrical purism and the inspiration of new techniques—nor any disrespect to the scientific approach that justifies this modern architecture's claim to be something more than an alternative style. But conscious though it may be of its social obligations, modern architecture has somehow never found the common touch. Whether in the course of time it can be trusted to do so, or how else it can manage to escape being led away into the unfruitful paths of private connoisseurship and technological narcissism, must be discussed in a later chapter. It is enough for the moment that the architectural theorists of today live in a world of regrets for the past and hopes about the future. Around them they see only chaos. Because they make the mistake of assuming that what is significant must bear the hall-mark of educated taste, they fail to observe that, not far beneath this chaotic surface, a common idiom of a kind does lie hidden, that which I have been speaking of as the suburban style.

This may not be the mature expressive idiom, the authentic voice of an age secure in its internal harmony, which these theorists, forgetful that such a voice cannot be expected to emerge prior to the establishment of such a harmony, are so anxiously anticipating. It is, moreover, confined to domestic architecture. But it has the one quality of all true vernaculars, that of being rooted in the people's instincts, and even its shortcomings—its snobberies, its self-deceptions, its sentimentalities, the uncertainties of its objectives—are evidence of this closeness to everyday life. The suburban style is part of the texture of the suburban world, which indeed is hardly aware of any other.

So there it is, our own contemporary vernacular, spread thinly but ubiquitously over English hill and dale—or what was hill and dale before the speculative builder or the municipal councillor so aptly interpreted the people's instincts and carpeted them with this intricate jungle of red peaked gables and evergreen hedges, multi-coloured chimneys and winding, tree-shaded avenues. From Becontree to Wythenshawe, from Port Sunlight to Angmering-on-Sea, the startling consistency of suburban character —despite its notorious vagaries in detail—indicates its origin in the living present. It could be the product of no other age than ours.

On account of its ubiquity alone we cannot afford to ignore it. During the twenty years between the two wars, four million new houses were built in England—enough to accommodate nearly a third of the population—and a very large proportion of these can be classed as suburban houses. So the suburban environment determines the style in which—for good or ill—modern England lives. But it is not its mere presence that is most significant; it is the universality of its appeal, to which I have already alluded. If democracy means anything, it means deciding —for a change—to pay some attention to the expressed preference of the majority, to what people themselves want, not what we think they ought to want. We may despise what they want. We may think they should be educated to want something different, or at least to know they could have something different if they wished, instead of their choice being limited by their ignorance of the alternatives; but we can only progress democratically at a speed which does not outpace the slow growth of the public's understanding, in particular its assimilation of social and technical change.

So, while continuing to build our castles in the air, let us not ignore those that already exist—somewhat untidily scattered, it is true—on the ground. In addition to searching the horizon for the promise of a new vernacular, let us accept also for what it is worth the one on our own doorstep. But what is it worth? In the pages that follow an attempt is made, taking the suburban style as an example of a idiom which, whatever its shortcomings, still has certain attributes essential to a true contemporary vernacular, to analyse these and discover the qualities on which the style's vernacular appeal rests.

One thing more should be said by way of introduction. If the suburban landscapes depicted in these pages seem idealized, the reader must remember that what is being set before him is the essence of the suburban environment, not the reality of every suburb. If every suburb is not so leafy or so opulent, that is because time and circumstances do not always allow the suburban ideal to be achieved. But the pilgrim to suburbia must go where the ideal has been most nearly achieved, and where it is preserved most fully flavoured. He, too, must be allowed his Broadway and his Bath, his discovery of an unspoilt world so all of a piece that no foot from any other world seems ever to have trodden there. Who enters such a paradise returns touched with some of its magic.

2

A Landscape from Within

The five words with which this book begins are meant to draw attention to an essential characteristic of the English suburb, that of being always carefully groomed. Indoors, this characteristic is not perhaps very remarkable, nor peculiarly English. The housewife in the industrial town is houseproud too. Remember the perspective of faultlessly whitened doorsteps down a long street of miners' cottages, the black-leaded grate in the parlour and the tiled kitchen floor scrubbed and polished so that you could eat a meal off it. Equally houseproud are the farmer's and the fisherman's wife, and—proverbially—their Dutch, their Danish and their German counterparts.

But in the English suburb the equivalent quality goes deeper than conscientious order and cleanliness. It is more positive, more creative, and, moreover, pervades both indoors and out, uniting them into a single world of its own making. The well-scrubbed floor is echoed in the well-mown lawn, the polished grate in the weeded gravel path, the Welsh dresser with its rows of gleaming plates in the vegetable bed where the purple sprouting broccoli is planted in equally meticulous rows, and each plant of the winter lettuce is carefully tied up with bass to keep even its outer leaves from drooping on to the damp or dusty ground. Care and cleanliness here recognise no difference between the house and its garden setting; Ewbank and Atco reign side by side.

The Englishman's passion for gardening may, it is true, be seen in other places than suburbia, but only here, in exercising this passion, does he create for himself an original world in which nothing is not subject to his determination and control. This is of profound significance, not merely because it is characteristic that, even at its peak of development, suburban luxuriance is never out of control, but because there follows from this the clue to the suburb's peculiar nature, that it is essentially synthetic.

The world the suburb creates, through the care and labour lavished on it, is an *ad hoc* world, conjured out of nothing. It is a mistake to think of the suburb as either the town spaced out or the country packed close. For the town evolves its shape from its function, from streets and squares and traffic intersections and the grouping of buildings, and the country from the adaptation of natural landscapes to human purposes. But the suburb is not primarily a mechanism, nor is it in any sense a modification of something previously existing; it is a world peculiar to itself and— as with a theatre's drop scene—before and behind it there is nothing.

From the synthetic nature of the suburb's origin thus comes the scenic nature of its appearance, and from the scenic nature of its appearance we get the first rule for looking at suburban architecture: to divest our minds of conventional judgments, which are based on what we regard as the architectural merits of individual buildings. We may then find that each suburban residence is not a self-sufficient piece of design but a contribution to a panoramic whole, and that its intrinsic architectural quality bears but small relation to the part it is capable of playing in building up the rich and varied picture which the suburb in its maturity comprises. The beefy redness of a tile-hung gable peeps with a certain effect above the foliage of syringa and juniper, lilac and laburnum, and it does so irrespective of the architectural refinement or otherwise of the gable *qua* gable. The mere suggestion of a silhouette of chimneys, hidden owing to a curve in the road behind a sycamore tree in the next-door garden, may prove to be of more value than the carefully studied roof-lines in the architect's perspective. The charm of the suburb, in fact, lies in its whole self. Just as the houses are furnished with stair-carpets, lampshades, umbrella stands and chests of drawers, so—inside and out being one—the suburban scene is itself furnished with an almost limitless variety of properties, in the shape of trees and shrubs, trellis-work and rockeries, oak-slatted gates and multi-faceted bay windows, and these are disposed and displayed with instinctive though unconscious skill.

This tradition of scene-painting, wherein the products of nature and of the builder are each made to play their part in producing, in an apparently casual way, an elaborately synthetic picture, is by no means a new one in English architecture. In fact it is in many senses identical with the English Picturesque tradition itself. Illustrations of this might be drawn from many times and many places. Let us take, as an instructive example, Nash's work at Regent's Park, London, if only because the Prince Regent's architect was, if not one of the first to approach architectural problems scenically, one of the first to suggest the scenic opportunities offered when relatively small units of domestic architecture were laid out as a single conception.

This is not to say that Regent's Park—or any other work of the same period—has a great deal in common with the romantic luxuriance of the English suburb as we now know it. It took fully a hundred years after Nash's day to develop that singular combination of individual assertiveness and instinctive self-efface-ment most characteristic of the twentieth-century suburban style, a combination which the Prince Regent's architectural megalo-mania and the deliberation with which the scenic effects of Nash's day were planned would have made impossible earlier. In a hundred years, too, the picturesqueness of treatment which Nash and his landscape-gardening predecessors brought to the surround-ings of their classical buildings, gave way to a picturesqueness of conception which merged the buildings and their settings into one. And at the same time the suburb's variety of fancy-dress styles, dependent for their effects as much on romantic associations as on sophisticated architectural design, supplanted the autumnal classic to which the Regency was still largely bound.

Such work as Nash's may however be said to be the link between the landscaped country park in which the Picturesque tradition

was born, and the garden suburb in which it met what some would call its decay but what might also be called its translation into another and less formal Picturesqueness, on a more intimate, domestic scale. Nash was already a romantic at heart; only the classical formulæ in which he dealt gave to his work, despite the lack of scholarship his purist critics have all too diligently noted, a deceptive air of continuity with the Augustan tradition.

The beginning of the romantic approach to, and the scenic treatment of, domestic layouts can be seen emerging very clearly in Nash's Regent's Park development. Set out on a winter's morning down the Broad Walk from Prince Albert Road, southwards towards that grey granite drinking fountain which an anglophile maharajah has so guilelessly dedicated to the people of London. On the left, over the undulating grass, glimpsed between the trunks and through the bare branches of well-grown park trees, are the long cream-coloured facades of several terraces. Gloucester Terrace, Cumberland Terrace, Chester Terrace, their somewhat sketchily designed stucco fronts, providing but one ingredient out of many—natural and architectural, animal, vegetable and mineral—from which the picture is composed, display themselves as on a scene-painter's backcloth. It is not one but a sequence of pictures, changing as the viewpoint shifts, now emphasizing the serrated skyline of statues, pediments, roofs and chimneys—strangely but significantly unclassical—now the screen of trees and shrubs behind which the pale facades glide into sight and out again like a two-dimensional architectural ghost, now the diminishing perspective of balustrades and pillared porches as the line of terraces curves round behind the bushy evergreens that line the Outer Circle. Only now and then do the cliff-like facades tell as solid self-sufficient architecture and remind us of their origin in the stucco mansion set in its landscaped park.

In this changing panorama we thus find a scenic treatment of a domestic architectural theme, but this is not what we have really come to see. Close by we can find the same line of development much further advanced, so much so that its relationship with the modern suburban style is quite easily identified. To see—in date only a few years later—the romance of domesticity frankly dominating the scenic lay-out, we only have to turn back a little way along the Broad Walk, cross the grass of the Park itself, making our way parallel with the now filled-in Regent's Canal, to the other side of Albany Street, and visit the small secluded colony of houses called Park Village West. Here the interdependence of building and garden setting has assumed three-dimensional form; it is no longer merely pictorial. Here is a prototype of something quite familiar. Romanticism has taken charge, and has broken down the flat terrace facades into a cunningly informal group of toy-like villas, each different in design and each set off against a background of trees and hedges. A curling road winds through them in true suburban style and—also in true suburban style—the impression we get of their architecture is no longer one of a panorama of buildings spread out before us, but of a changing view of roof-slopes, oriels and turrets, half concealed by the thickly planted vegetation and viewed from a succession of odd angles as each villa comes into view round the next corner of the circular road.

Only the cream-painted stucco, and the predominance of certain architectural mannerisms, link Park Village in time with the neighbouring terraces, whose somewhat squalid backs of greyish brick face the exit from the green recesses of Park Village on the other side of Albany Street. Here is physical proof that Nash, who conceived Park Village, and Pennethorne, his pupil who executed it, did have some previsions of the secluded romantic environment the residential suburb was one day to make peculiarly its own. Nash himself, on another occasion, moved one stage nearer still. Far away from Regent's Park, at Blaise Castle near Bristol, he built in 1811 a model hamlet in a similarly romantic vein, lavishly planted and furnished with rustic cottages grouped with deceptively casual informality round a little green. The architecture is predominantly Tudor, but there is a fanciful mingling of many rustic styles, and for the first time appear those glimpses of tiled roof-peaks, chimneys and gables peeping out from behind tree and hedgerow that have become familiar in later generations and now stand as the insignia of Metroland itself.

Let us not, however, set too much store by Nash or any other individuals in whose work we find aspects of the suburban style anticipated. Neither he nor they were in any personal sense the inventors of the scenic approach to domestic architecture. Their romanticism was only one of the symptoms of the break-up of the classical tradition. It was part of a defiant movement which surged throughout a world that felt it was losing its equilibrium, and felt at the same time a need to make some protest against that matter-of-factness which had become the sole residue of the exciting Renaissance discovery of the material world. In some senses the wheel has now come full circle, and romantic ideals once more preoccupy a world uncertain of its allegiances; but our own romanticism is not entirely a revival of that of a century ago, if only because the latter has never quite vanished. In the longest perspectives of history, today and that comparatively recent yesterday belong to the same epoch, the post-Renaissance epoch, and by a long-drawn process which is still not ended, what began—architecturally speaking—as a somewhat irresponsible gesture has matured into a consistent attitude of mind, which can be seen more clearly reflected in the suburb than elsewhere. Indeed before the onset of romanticism suburbia did not even exist. In this maturing process some—but by no means all—of the element of fantasy which we find in the earlier romanticism may have gone, but the spirit of make-believe remains, that spirit having, however, a social rather than an architectural basis, as we shall presently see.

In its romantic aspect, as in many others, the history of the suburb is a fascinating study, but in this book I am less concerned with the suburb's past than with what it is like at present and how it fits physically into the pattern of our civilization. So I will leave it to someone else to follow in detail the architectural development of the English suburb through the nineteenth and early twentieth centuries, and describe how successive influences and examples contributed to its growth: how William Morris first translated into architectural terms the urge to escape from the grim squalor of the industrial slums; how a genteel rusticity was idealized in the water-colours of Birket Foster; how patriarchal industrialists found in the new suburban style a fitting vehicle for their new humanitarianism, producing therefrom Bournville, Port Sunlight and the rest; how the drab aridity of Turnham Green blossomed miraculously into Bedford Park, the pioneer of planned suburbs, and how its architect Norman Shaw rediscovered the rich variety of materials and textures traditional to the English farmhouse; how the small English house, under the same rustic influence and in the hands of Voysey, Ernest Newton and Baillie Scott, broke forth from the box-like Regency villa into a looser, more casual arrangement of plan, a more informal grouping of roofs, initiating the process of linking house and garden together; how this almost accidental innovation took the Continent by storm and was worshipped as a shining light brought into the darkness of architectural scholasticism, so that der '*Cottage*' *Stil* became a synonym for a new spirit in architecture and the rising tide of romantic domesticity deposited a scattering of red-roofed villas set among flowering shrubberies in the outskirts of mid-European cities and Riviera watering-places, where bougainvillea and oleander give a strange exotic flavour to porches and pathways customarily adorned with hollyhocks or the climbing English rose; how, back home again, the fashion for conservatories and gravel drives was succeeded by the fashion for rockeries and crazy paving; how the motor-car and the motor-bus picked up the houses of the city workers from around the railway station and sprinkled them over the nearby country, along old roads and new; how the Garden City was invented by Ebenezer Howard as an inspiring social theory but declined, through repeated emphasis on inessentials, into a retreat for cranks and a subject for the misplaced enthusiasm of the well-intentioned; how the rapacity of speculative builders speeded up the growth of suburbs and somewhat diluted the rich mixture which was fermenting slowly and sedately towards maturity of style; and how municipalities took a hand and pinned their elusive victim perhaps too firmly to the drawing boards of their town-planning offices, but how even the municipalized suburb managed to retain its vitality despite the deadening influence of bye-law observance.

But that is all past history. The suburb in which we are interested is a living thing, continually revitalized as it responds to social urges in the immediate present. Having made our obeisance to Regent's Park, an example of scenic architecture still tied to classical formality and catering for a decaying social hierarchy, and to Blaise hamlet, a tentative and somewhat self-conscious example of drawing-room rusticity, let us leap a hundred years at once to the suburb of mature vintage, the well-grown article of our fathers' generation.

If we take a walk down a road in one of these well-matured suburbs, what sort of panorama unfolds itself to us? The word 'unfold' is used advisedly, because the panorama is always changing; it is not a static one, as my analogy with stage scenery may have suggested. Like the theatre stage, it is a self-contained world furnished with a number of properties of a kind and variety that together make up what I am calling the suburban style. But it is not a flat backcloth; it is a panorama in depth as well as breadth and therefore shows itself in continually new aspects as the spectator moves before it. Instead of facing the scene from beyond the footlights, or even from the stage itself, our pilgrim to suburbia must be thought of as having somehow stepped inside it. In the same way that Alice, dreaming in front of the looking-glass, found herself translated into the world beyond it, or that a child, gazing through the eye-hole of a Victorian peep-show, might imagine himself suddenly projected within the box, with its strange brightly coloured world all round him, so the pilgrim visiting suburbia finds he is no longer looking at the picture from outside. The well-furnished scene has become a kind of well-stocked jungle—not a fearsome one, because stocked with tame trees, tame houses and tame gardens—but one from which all other worlds are shut out.

The Castles on the Ground

Suburbia has closed in round him, and is so completely a world of its own that it is the untidy, incalculable city from which he has come, or the countryside with its frightening expanse of sky, that seem strange and unreal.

The capacity of unfolding itself gradually to the spectator who has penetrated within it leads to another characteristic of the suburban style, its use of concealment and surprise. Not everything is revealed at once; straight roads do not separate two pictures, viewed independently according as you look to right or left. Instead, winding roads penetrate a single three-dimensional picture, and new objects or groupings of objects are constantly hidden and revealed: a chimney for but a moment here, a turret window through this gap between two acacia trees, a gable partly concealed by the fretted roof of this foreground conservatory, an almond tree in blossom, branching over the pavement down that side turning, which itself curves out of sight before we have seen what else it contains, a spot of scarlet colour made by a distant pillar box. The infinite variety of such effects is the chief basis of the suburb's elusive charm.

This characteristic points back once more to the suburb's origin in the English Picturesque tradition and the English school of landscape gardening, where concealment and surprise were also exploited and full account was taken of the spectator's changing viewpoint. But in those days it was all contrived and calculated, and the fact that the modern suburban style can produce similar effects casually and as if by instinct is further proof that we have in it something resembling a genuine vernacular. It is one of the attributes of a vernacular that its characteristic effects are not produced selfconsciously but through the operation of an instinctive sense of style, and suburban architecture at its best may therefore be said to represent the true vernacular development of the Picturesque landscape tradition, in the same way that Georgian farm buildings and market squares represent the true vernacular development of the tradition of scholarship and taste established by Wren and the architects who followed him.

A Landscape from Within

It is interesting to observe, however, that the suburban style looks forward as well as back. Its essentially three-dimensional quality is of course a quality common to all good architecture when it is not bound by the discipline of urban street frontages. But here it means not only that roads wind freely within suburbia's jungle landscapes, and not only that, by means of that characteristic suburban invention the 'front' garden, the rigid demarcation of the street has disappeared as an element in the picture; it means also, to some degree, the penetration of house by garden and garden by house, forecasting the ultimate breaking down of the outer wall, a tendency particularly identified with modern architecture. Such a tendency derives naturally from the tradition of rustic informality which I have already mentioned as having been revived with such effect in the small English house of the late nineteenth century.

It also derives from new structural techniques, especially skeleton construction which substitutes a few points of support for continuous solid walls, and therefore allows the house to break free from its walls' confining influence. But this last technical development in architecture has in practice hardly yet made its mark on the suburb, since the suburb is not yet ready to exploit it—it should never be forgotten that technical innovations do not appear out of the blue, but only when some need is already there to nourish them. The sense in which the instinctive needs of the suburb do not yet allow the full implications of certain modern technical developments—this among them—to be fully made use of, must be left for discussion later, but the ideal is unmistakably there. The oneness of indoors and out, as already defined at the beginning of this chapter in terms of the equal carefulness with which both are tended, exists in embryo in an architectural sense also. Now and then, indeed, glimpses of it are encountered in reality, as when we get an unexpected view past an open front door right through the house into the garden at the back, whose sub-aqueous greenness seems intensified by being framed in the dark interior, or when we see from an upper window a pattern of small suburban gardens, parcelled out like a series of outdoor rooms, and themselves subdivided further by thick hedges, creeper-covered trellises and green walls of vegetables entwined on poles. We encounter it most of all, perhaps, when we step inside a conservatory, that ubiquitous feature in the suburban landscape, and find how it has brought under one glittering roof the attributes of house and garden in a significantly artificial way.

These, then, are the special qualities the observant pilgrim is able to distinguish in the suburban style: it is an *ad hoc* world, created rather than evolved; it concerns itself first of all with scenic effects, which outweigh strictly architectural considerations; these scenic effects depend on depth as well as breadth, and on a sense in the observer of being within the dense suburban jungle, not outside it; and it relies much on the romantic technique of concealment and surprise, of charms enhanced because they are grudgingly revealed. Finally, to counterbalance the suburb's instinct for panoramic effect, there is also a more conscious and personal interest in detail of every kind. This is reflected in the kind of picture we have in our minds when we recall any suburb we have known. We generally let a single scene—any one of those casually revealing glimpses which I have described as typical of the suburban style of landscape—or a single object, represent the whole for us; something, whatever it is, in which we ourselves can concentrate more significance than it contains for everyone. This is quite in character with the other suburban qualities; for it is the nature of romanticism to fasten on to the particular rather than on to general statements, to react to the stimulus of *things* and glorify what the sensibilities can seize hold of while the abstract impersonal world flings by. But this introduces another topic, that of what the architecture of the suburb means to the people who live in it, which is the subject of the next chapter.

3

The Anatomy of Suburbia

So far we have discussed only the pictorial aspect of the suburb. In dealing with a visual art it is proper to begin with that which meets the eye, and it is a commonplace of criticism that architecture should be judged by what it is physically, and not thought better of—or worse of—according to what the critic may happen to know of the intentions behind it. But we are interested in analysing as well as admiring the suburban style, and in wider issues than strictly architectural ones; so we must look at it socially as well as pictorially.

We have also discussed the suburb so far only as the outsider sees it; the next thing to do is to have a look at it from the point of view of the people who inhabit it. Let us therefore leave our pilgrim to continue his explorations of suburbia alone for the time being. He will be used to finding himself alone, since he is a rare enough animal in this jungle, it being a characteristic of the suburban world that it keeps itself to itself and seldom receives visitors from worlds outside. The countryman comes up to town— he is to be seen any day, one is told, with a straw in his mouth, standing agape in Piccadilly Circus—and the townsman goes to the country, to hike up Derbyshire dales or spend weekends in cottages in damp Sussex woods. But neither of them ever makes an expedition into suburbia. They little know what they would find there.

We have already described the suburb as being of the suburban dweller's own making. He is not only master in his own house but creator of his own world. And this creation is a process in which he has a very personal share. The town and the countryside are man-made too, but they are the impersonal product of a collective effort, whereas in the suburb each man can see his own handiwork. It may be only a rockery he has built or a tree of his own planting which he can see over-topping the hedge as he turns the corner of the road on his return from the city in the evening, but to some extent he can feel responsible for his environment and thus get a sense of controlling his destiny.

Here we have a clue to much that is puzzling in the suburban scene, and particularly to the origins of suburban architectural taste. The thing which is familiar is felt to be the more governable —'better the devil you know than the devil you don't know'—and at least some of the appeal that suburban architecture makes is to the conservative instinct which clings to whatever can be trusted not to introduce new uncertainties into an existence already uncertain enough. This is true not only in the obvious sense that it makes for a general unwillingness to change, but also in the sense that it makes for an instinctive preference for architectural styles which themselves help to create an atmosphere of permanence and security.

The times we live in do not provide much sense of security for the individual. He is increasingly the victim of circumstances beyond his control. This particularly applies to the middle and artisan classes, by whom the suburbs are chiefly populated. Besides the fear of actual want, which may or may not be present and is less likely to be so today than it was in the nineteenth century, when society had taken no steps at all to cope with the evils brought about by commercial industrialism, there is also the fear of sinking to a lower social level than that which parents or grandparents have left behind as their most precious legacy; or, if not that, of somehow failing in the struggle for prestige and betterment which the uncertainties of the world have caused to play such an exaggerated part in social relationships.

This struggle is primarily an economic one. The partial removal of the fear of actual want has not removed the social stigma attached to poverty, so there is an additional incentive to keep up appearances and to do so through the well-tried means of architectural symbolism. Thus we get the snobberies of suburban architectural styles, the significance attached to the separate tradesman's entrance, the perpetuation of the subtle difference between the wooden paling and the privet hedge, between plain rough-cast ('looks like a Council House') and imitation oak beams. Architectural styles have to be reinterpreted as social symbols. An elaborate code has grown up, instinctively understood by those whom it concerns, by means of which family circumstances are depicted and achievements recorded in architectural language, almost after the fashion of heraldry. Advantageous alliances are reflected as clearly in a fructification of shrubberies and bay windows as they are in elaborate quarterings, and a Council cottage may carry the same degree of obloquy as a bar sinister.

The first instinct, however, of the suburban dweller is his craving for economic security, and, in a world that does not provide this, for a defence that is always close at hand against the knowledge that he is at the mercy of elements which he cannot in the least control. That he is able to take refuge from the implications of such knowledge in the domestic charms of a manufactured environment is a tribute to his typically English capacity for hand-to-mouth happiness and to his optimism, a virtue which far outweighs the concomitant vice of self-deception.

Another such tribute, of a more particular kind, is the success of the Building Societies in persuading the suburban dweller how desirable it is for him to own his own home. See the advertisements in which the earnest father, his pipe in his mouth, perhaps a fox terrier at his feet, his arm round the shoulders of his handsome son, gazes (with all the pride of the squire regarding his ancestral acres) at a cosy villa such as Metroland breeds by the thousand. 'One day', he is saying, 'it will be ours.' It is ironical enough that the fear of economic insecurity should be held at bay by the idea of the acquisition of property, which can have no result but to bind the owner more firmly to the economic machine of which he is the victim rather than the operator, but his reaction is a natural one. It is in keeping with his ambition to take root, to reduce his responsibilities to a kind his eye and mind can encompass, to contrive for himself an environment—even though a make-believe one —in which he is master. And, as though in direct answer to all such ambitions, there is the suburban style in the act of echoing the country squire's own tradition-rooted architecture; there are the red roofs and chimneys—or a caricature of them, if you like—of manorial England, the smooth lawns and lattice windows belonging to the good old times when the immediate world was a self-sufficient place, when the world beyond the horizon could be ignored and a slump on the New York stock exchange did not result in the sudden dismissal of numberless bread-winners from their employment at Middlesbrough or Nottingham or West Drayton. It is all too clear why the outside world is barred as far as possible from intrusion into the suburban jungle.

It may have seemed, when we were painting our somewhat idyllic picture of the suburb's outward charms, of its winding tree-lined roads and its glimpses into well-tended gardens with all the architectural appurtenances of cosy domesticity beyond, that we too easily explained away the bad reputation it has among people who know what's what by saying that its architecture must not be criticised piecemeal but only in relation to what it contributes to the pictorial whole. It is not necessary, however, to leave it at that, and the reason why suburban architecture, especially in the strict sense of the design of buildings and groups of buildings, has been left for discussion until this moment is now perhaps apparent: there may or may not be such a thing as an absolute in architecture generally, but at least it can be said of suburban architecture in particular that it can only be properly understood in the light of the instincts and ideals, sentimentalities and snobberies, which form the basis of the twentieth-century suburban world. The economic origin of these has already been suggested; in a world made unsafe for self-sufficiency, suburban architecture can be described as an attempt to create a kind of oasis in which every tree and every brick can be accounted for, to exclude the unpredictable as far as possible from everyday life. This factor,

I think, explains much of what we find typical of the suburban style, and reinforcing it—leading suburban architecture still more surely towards the various fancies it delights to indulge in—is another factor, the romantic idealism already spoken of, in which the whole suburban landscape is saturated. This is in part, of course, only a further escape from the brutalities of the day-to-day world, but it is also an expression of the urge to escape from materialism itself. In this latter sense, it has already been suggested, the suburban romanticism of our day is one with that of a hundred and a hundred and fifty years ago.

We are still living in the post-Renaissance period, a period which has always been preoccupied—consciously or unconsciously —with the need for knowledge and beliefs capable of reaching beyond the hard facts of science. It was the achievement of the Renaissance that it gave a rational basis to civilization; for medieval faith it substituted demonstrable proofs, for superstition a healthy scepticism, for subservience to the Church the perfection of secular organization. The invention of the art of perspective in fifteenth-century Italy may have been merely the outcome of scientific inquisitiveness, but it can also stand as a symbol of an attitude of mind that demands an explanation and a place for all things, and is no longer content for phenomena to appear out of the earth, in foreground or background, as by the will of God. The Renaissance insistence on the rational does not of course indicate an absence of spirituality, for the field of knowledge was then so open, the excitement of discovery, of piecing together the jig-saw puzzle of a newly revealed world, was so intense, that it served as a spiritual driving force, illuminating material progress with a new kind of disinterested faith.

But man having discovered himself, and having placed himself in a grand perspective of law and order, cause and effect, the physical world lost its exciting quality. Progress became less disinterested; science hitched its wagon not to a star but to a line of coal trucks, and man's spiritual needs demanded a new, less tangible, outlet. This is one explanation of the romantic strivings of the eighteenth and nineteenth centuries, including those some-times rather absurd efforts to recapture the spirit of such previous ages as had never been enslaved by material standards: efforts to revive Gothic architecture or the merchant guilds or herbal medi-cine or the mysteries of ritual worship. Similarly linked with the search for more natural and primitive things than materialism provides are many other phenomena of the nineteenth and twen-tieth centuries, not forgetting the kind of romantic idealism that dominates the suburban environment and flourishes in the leafy recesses of the suburban world.

Occasionally the nineteenth century, it is true, found itself recapturing the excitement of discovery that had constantly revitalized and spiritualized the material progress of the Renais-sance, as in the railway building age or the age of new experiment in iron and steel; hence the genuine reverence with which great machines were regarded, and hence the nobility of the work of the great engineers of the early nineteenth century, who, being in-spired by a real creative instinct, brought imagination to reinforce the practical worth of their engineering achievements. But the Victorian age, in spite of the hard-headed Victorian industrialist, of the scientist who looked no further than his laboratory bench and of the politician who made Free Trade his gospel, was in general a romantic age, lacking only a philosophy capable of em-bracing both the scientific and spiritual worlds on which it could have based a recreation of its faith. Our own age, pending some unforeseeable fusion of romance and reality into one, bears the same character and is perplexed by the same divergent instincts.

After this rather necessary excursion into history, as it determines the cultures of succeeding generations, let us return to the physical fact of the English suburb. What we can hope to find there is not that elusive and unnecessary chimera, absolute architectural merit, but evidence that it gives to the people who live in it some of the things that they, in their circumstances, demand from their en-vironment; in particular, two things: a sense of belonging to a fairly sympathetic world and an opportunity of making out of that world something personal to themselves—in fact an outlet for their idealistic and creative instincts.

These two things might be called the negative and the positive roles of the suburban environment respectively, since one is concerned with shutting out an unkind world and the other is actively concerned with putting something—be it only a mirage or a facade of make-believe—in its place. And all criticism must take into account the limitations set by these two roles. When considering suburbia's negative (or escapist) aspects, for example, we must not expect the enterprise appropriate to a mind that looks outward at an expanding world with confidence in its own relation to it; we must expect qualities more appropriate to a mind that looks secretively inward in search of a world where an illusion of security can be obtained by grasping hold of whatever may serve as an anchorage to the past. When considering its positive aspect, we must remember that it is the creative outlet that matters most. The special conditions that must exist before the exercise of the creative instinct can produce something on whose intrinsic goodness everyone can agree must be discussed later. They were hinted at in the concluding words of the paragraph before last.

But we are straying once more from the physical fact of the suburb itself. We are tempted to do so because, as we look at it, our first feeling is one of bewilderment at its variety, and in our search for some common denominator we fall back on generalizations, usually of a critical kind. But when we have decided that these generalizations are not really applicable to the case, do we find the variety so bewildering after all? If we accept fantasy— and the sense of release that fantasy offers—as an end in itself, is not the suburban landscape one the world over, and is not its very variety the hallmark that proves its authenticity?

To illustrate our arguments up till now we have used the fairly prosperous suburb of about half a century ago. There we saw architectural anarchy mellowed by time into a single style which seemed to be all of a piece. One reason why it seems all of a piece to our eyes is that all the elements—miscellaneous though they may be—of which it is composed have associations for us with the same period in history; we have become accustomed to seeing them as parts of the same picture. Nevertheless, when this suburb was new these elements must have appeared as completely unrelated to each other as the elements that compose a modern suburb do now. Anarchy, in fact, is the basis of the suburban style, and the influence of time and posterity plays a large part in giving them whatever unity we of today find in the earlier suburbs.

A further part is, of course, played by that romantic instinct, already discussed, which demands that the treatment of the whole suburban landscape shall be a scenic one rather than a piecemeal architectural one. The richly endowed suburb of the nineties has already been described as a kind of jungle, furnished with everything in the way of turrets and gables, shrubberies and conservatories, unexpected crannies and enticing green vistas necessary to enable it to create its own secretive world. This jungle is all of a piece; it is only the architect's eye that picks out incongruities of style and misleads him into condemning it for its failure in knowledge and taste. But taste has not failed, because taste was never exercised. The style is a builder's vernacular, composed out of the elements the builder found at hand when he came to build. The turrets and gables current in the nineties were the raw material out of which the suburban fantasies were inevitably woven. Builders have always done the same. It is not they who invent styles any more than it is the man in the street who discriminates about them. That is left to the expert—the man of taste—who comes along afterwards.

In this respect the old and the new suburb are one. The new one, like the old, is not an assemblage of architectural designs but a fantasy woven from the vernacular elements that the ebb and the flow of the tide of fashion have left convenient to the builder's hand. It is admittedly less easy to admire the modern suburb than the old one, and to credit it with the same consistency of style. People who are willing to admit the charm of the latter, for the sake of its atmosphere and the kind of sanctity with which time and the

cycle of romantic taste are now beginning to invest its architecture, can often do nothing but condemn the former. For in these modern suburbs, especially in the case of the most newly constructed of all, instead of our well-groomed landscape, so cunningly contrived so that all other worlds shall be excluded, we find a barren acreage of bricks and mortar within which the chilly atmosphere of the outside world circulates all too freely. On the surface we find a mere inhabited locality, but if we look closer—and especially if we allow for the absence of that mellowness and unity which only time will bring—we will find that old and new have more in common than we think. In the earlier suburb emphasis is laid on what I have called suburbia's negative role—the escapist one—and we are easily seduced by the period charm which serves this purpose so well. But the newer suburb is still too closely tied to the busy world to be so good for purposes of escape. It has to fulfil its function by playing a positive role; its success depends on the opportunities for fantasy it can help to create out of its own resources, unhelped by the charms which time will add. And the trouble is that, in the absence of these charms, we do not always recognize successful fantasy even when it has been achieved. Only when suburban fantasy has matured into a recognizable style and we are able to observe how it embodies the history of a passing mode of life in its outward being, do we give it full credit at the same time as we give it a period label.

The fantasy, *qua* fantasy, while it is in process of creation in the modern suburb, is more difficult to recognize. Nevertheless it remains one of the few outlets available to that portion of society which, in the modern world, finds itself generally deprived of outlets for its creative instinct. How a whole section of society comes to find itself in this situation lies outside the scope of this book, so let us turn back once more to the suburb itself. There we can study the creation of fantasy in daily operation, having established the principle that it does not matter very much if the things we find to interest us outrage the taste of those for—and by— whom books about architecture are generally written.

4

Another Man's Poison

We can take the train from any metropolitan terminus, the same train, steam or electric, in which the civil servant, the artisan, the business man and his typist, make their daily journey to the busy world and back again. Six return journeys a week they make. On Sunday the trains are empty, for that is the day when the suburb comes into its own. On Sunday the inhabitants remain to worship the suburban gods according to their special ritual, and with all the sights and sounds that accompany it—the sounds especially: the music of lawn-mowers, the snip-snip of garden shears, the barking of small dogs straining to be let off the leash at the first turning off the main road, the squeals of a child who is being taught to ride a bicycle down the second quiet turning, the roaring exhaust as a girl friend is whisked off for the day in a sports car and the high-pitched chatter of the group that swings its racquets gaily as it strides in line abreast across the pavement on its way to the tennis club—a group of three only, the observer may notice, but this is because one of their number has bustled on ahead as it is her turn to prepare the teas, to get the urn going and make the cucumber sandwiches. Preoccupation with these and many other private activities, and indeed the very somnolence of shady streets and the shuttered fronts of shops, result in a barrier being erected between suburbia and the outside world which only Monday morning's alarm clock can break down again.

We ourselves begin to penetrate this barrier when our train draws up at the station to which we have taken our ticket. We are at once surrounded by familiar, well-loved objects that give its local colour to the suburban scene; to begin with, the tin-plated

42

advertisements for Mazawattee Tea and Iron Jelloids and Stephens' Ink. Passengers must not cross the line except by the bridge, and we shall see the second of these advertisements only when we do so, because it adorns each riser of the stairs up which we have to climb, but the spectacular blot of Stephens' Ink catches our eye almost before the train has stopped moving. Then there are the slot machines, some with five compartments containing exotic products like caramels and throat pastilles as well as the usual chocolate. Perhaps a lad is idly pulling at the trays on the chance that someone has been improvident enough to put in a penny without claiming his prize, though why anyone should do so he would not know if you asked him. There is W. H. Smith's paper stall, open on week-day mornings only, now closed behind a rolling shutter. There is the local photographer's showcase, filled with simpering bridesmaids and petulant children dressed only in a wisp of chiffon they certainly did not bring with them and clutching a teddy-bear they are hoping they will be allowed to take away. There are advertisements of the local nursing home and of a tea-shop that specializes in home-made cakes, the second a hand-painted one decorated with ladies in crinolines. But we must not dally among the delights of the railway station, except to note in passing how hard it is to draw the line between the period charm of the old-fashioned and the contemporary charm of what is sharply characteristic. It is typical of the suburban scene, in fact, that it is an accumulation of trivialities; the novelties of this year are always being added to the novelties of last year, and these are always fading into insignificance until they are ready to emerge again in the character of the old and familiar things that we wondered at in childhood. All is grist to this mill, as we see when we emerge from the station. Half-way up the station approach is a shabby shed-like building, the coal merchant's office, with a window containing baskets of Best Kitchen Nuts and Derby Brights, and near it the only remaining four-wheeled cab waits for the rare aged passenger. But at the bottom of the approach stands the new Odeon super cinema, glamorous in chromium plate.

The Castles on the Ground

If we turn left here we find ourselves walking downhill along a wide stretch of pavement, past a row of shops. These shops are probably called simply The Parade. They are not quite so new as the Odeon, though some of them have had their facades brought up to date with jazz lettering and plate glass windows of the kind where the glass is not framed but butts at right angles, the sheets being joined by a metal clip. There is a dress shop like this, called 'Mary's', with a sparsely dressed window, containing only one or two garments draped on aluminium stands and leaving the interior of the shop visible beyond a low, pleated curtain; also a wireless shop, very untidy by contrast, both inside and out, but one that has gone to the expense of a neon sign over the door. The branch of Boots has also been lately refronted, but it does not look so new because of the curly lettering on the gilt and glass fascia-board and the old-fashioned way the windows are packed with every kind of goods. In contrast to these are one or two shops that have clearly been there a long time, notably a dairy with a window surrounded by yellow, green and white tiles in an *art nouveau* pattern and containing a large polished brass milk-churn, whose flamboyant inscription is worn into illegibility with much rubbing. This churn is flanked by two china statuary groups of milkmaids, farm-boys, jersey cows and well-fed sheep dogs in pastel shades of rose, sea-green and cocoa-brown. The interior of the shop is rather dark but cool looking, its old-fashioned air a little spoilt by an ice-cream counter just within the door that blatantly advertises cornets.

There is no need to describe the other shops in The Parade: the draper's, a thriving business but old-fashioned compared with Mary's—its windows are hung with all sorts of garments and miscellaneous stuffs—where you could always buy *broderie anglaise* during the time it was too dowdy to be obtainable in the West End, more than one tobacconist and sweetshop, and a branch of the International Stores, in front of which stands a triangular framework in which customers can leave their bicycles.

When the suburb was first built The Parade was its only row

of shops. This was long before the days of the municipal 'shopping centre' put up in 1928 in connection with the new estate half a mile to the east, the one where shopkeepers kept on going bankrupt because housewives were at first too conservative to patronise them, even though by doing so they could save themselves the long walk to The Parade. It was also, of course, before the days when shops sprang up along the new by-pass road where it crosses the continuation of the High Street at the top of the hill. Old residents, in fact, still do not acknowledge these shops as part of the suburb; they really belong to the world of by-pass roads where motorists only halt for petrol as they chase each other to the sea. If we travel to the suburb by car instead of by train, we do not enter it when we reach the cross-roads, although by then we are officially within its boundaries. We must turn down the hill till we are within sight of the green trees that line the pavement at the bottom, where the road dodges round the church. Then we will feel the difference at once; we are less exposed now—within the suburb and not outside it.

The shops in The Parade, then, for many of its inhabitants—especially the older ones—are a centre of the gregarious weekday life of the suburb. Housewives come almost every morning, visiting them in regular order, exchanging the gossip of the day as they meet and part and meet again further down the hill. To the younger generation they are also an important centre, full of memories and associations: memories of standing in front of the sweetshop window at an age when one's chin barely reached the sill, of the bad luck when, on a hot summer's day, one passed the dairy on the opposite side of the road and had no chance to plead for an ice-cream cornet, of the unendurable boredom of sitting in the gloom of the draper's on one of those tall stools that almost toppled over if one fidgeted, wondering how anyone could take so long to make up their mind, of one's first puncture repair outfit, of the enticing smell that came out of the tobacconist's, and so on for every age and season, until one achieved sufficient independence to spend one's pocket money and leisure entertaining friends to indigestible teas at the Odeon, where the café over the foyer was a favourite rendezvous. This café was an immediate success when it opened. Like the outside of the cinema it displayed plenty of chromium plate and tubular lighting, but there were also wicker chairs and tables painted green, cleverly shaded with gold, and a jazz-pattern carpet and a soda fountain in Spanish Colonial style.

There is thus some part of The Parade that holds memories for everyone and appeals to everyone's taste. This taste, it is true, is partly a matter of memory; that is to say, it is partly based on familiarity. But it also moves with the times, and here we might halt our voyage of discovery for a moment and see what the contrasts we find in The Parade can tell us about that important phenomenon the cycle of taste. 'Taste' is a word we have tried to avoid using hitherto, because taste implies the superiority of one thing over another, and we were at pains to point out that relative merit does not arise when we are studying the differences that different ideals naturally produce. We are concerned with what the suburban resident really likes, as distinct from what sophisticated people think he ought to like, and if we can assume that the evolution of his preference is at least partially illustrated by what we find in The Parade, we can say that the most marked contrast is that between the dairy and the Odeon. The latter is absolutely the last word, but when the former was built it was the last word too; so much so that its *art nouveau* tiling shocked nearly everyone when it first intruded itself into this respectable row of red brick and terra-cotta shop fronts, relieved in those days only by soberly painted woodwork and a modest amount of polished brass. Since then, the same dairy, itself unchanged, has no doubt passed through each of the successive stages of public regard and disparagement that together form the so-called cycle of taste.

Perhaps cycle of popularity would be a better term. First the dairy was new-fangled, then fashionable, then merely commonplace, then rather dowdy, then laughably old-fashioned and out of date, then (to the sophisticated) attractively 'period', and so on.

Another Man's Poison

This last one is probably as advanced a stage as will be reached for a little while, and to the ordinary suburban resident—the non-sophisticate—the dairy is still in the previous stage; it is still merely an old-fashioned type of shop with no romance attached to it. For him the next stage will have arrived when it is generally acknowledged to be romantically old-world. The final stage is, one supposes, its acceptance and veneration as a museum piece.

This last category is by definition a more elusive one than the others, and entry into it will be dependent on certain conditions. Exactly what these conditions are would be difficult to define at the present time, since we are only just arriving at the unprecedented moment when products of the modern age begin to qualify for the later stages of the cycle of popularity. Hitherto we have only seen the complete cycle in operation as regards the products of the handicraft age, which acquire a rarity value with the lapse of time or have unique qualities of craftsmanship to recommend them. Now that the products of the factory system—which means mass production as well as the more frequent use of synthetic materials—will soon have been in existence long enough to qualify as period pieces, the quantity in which they survive is alone likely to change the view posterity ultimately takes of them. But in any case we are not interested here in their ultimate elevation to the status of a museum piece, because this process will lift them out of the suburban environment and offer them to the judgment of posterity as a whole. In that exalted sphere taste can afford to claim alliance with merit, and the economic and social influences we see at work in the suburb will no longer apply. Sufficient for us is the progress of our *art nouveau* dairy up to the moment when it shows signs of acquiring a new period interest, having survived the doldrums of dowdiness.

The whole cycle of popularity, indeed, is only of interest to us in so far as it suggests the large part played by the mere lapse of time in determining what we find ourselves ready to admire and what to condemn. If the sophisticated world is now almost ready to admire the *art nouveau* dairy again, will it not in due course admire the chromium bedecked Odeon too? Already there are signs that the day is coming when the older suburbs, recently despised, will be commonly admired. After the lapse of the necessary time the charm of their peeping gables and balustraded porches set among varied and intricate greenery will suddenly flash upon us, as full of romance as the manors and dower houses whose styles they emulate. And in due course will not the newer suburbs follow suit: the sham half-timbered villas with their creosoted garages, their crazy paving and the bottle glass in the panes of their front doors, and even the modernistic villas with corner windows, horizontal window panes, angular balconies and green glazed tiles on their roofs? At present, as in raw double lines they crawl up the half-made roads, like so many dolls' houses spilled out of a sack, they may seem to do nothing but brutally scar the surface of downland and meadow, but here too will time not have its way?

However, that is the outsider's viewpoint once again—and the superior outsider at that. The suburban world, less confused by aspirations towards the absolute and less self-conscious about the snobbery of good taste, likes the Odeon *now*, and the rows of dolls' house villas march across the meadow towards a goal about which no misgivings are felt. Let the people of taste, however, who look at suburbia from the outside and claim that what they admire is in some way 'better' than what they do not admire, take note of how much even their discriminating admiration is influenced by the lapse of time. How little reason, therefore, have they to impose their taste on the suburbs as something absolute, let alone as something relevant to the suburb's purposes.

Another thing to be noted—a thing which we find exemplified in The Parade—is that the cycle of popularity exists at all stages simultaneously. It takes all sorts to make the suburban world, and its essential quality lies in a mixture of familiarity and novelty, glamour and homeliness. The suburb is neither the refuge of dowdiness, tolerated for the sake of old associations, nor the playground of slick modernity, but is something of both and everything in between. The past jostles the present and pigeon-hole conventions are no more often true than untrue. Familiarity breeds no contempt, liberty does not lead to license and the new wine improves in the old bottles into which it is consistently being decanted.

To see this aspect of suburbia clearly we must get closer to its heart than our voyage of discovery has so far taken us; in fact we must penetrate inside the suburban home, for in its home life the impulses that dominate the suburban environment naturally have their origin. So down the hill that drops steeply from the lower end of The Parade, and round the corner where the road swerves to the left to avoid the church, which occupies a sort of mound, rising behind an old brick wall. It is quite an old church, though over-restored, built of brick and flint with a stumpy lead-covered spire, but we do not see much of it as we pass; it is mostly hidden by the lime trees and shrubby yews that grow in the graveyard, the former making a shady avenue out of the path that climbs up to the church porch from the elaborate tiled and timbered lych-gate which was put up as a memorial after the last war. With the lych-gate at our backs we begin to climb again. On our left, where the road widens somewhat as though it had half a mind to blossom into a village green (there is even an oldish tree, ringed with an iron railing, planted on the edge of the pavement), is the Fire Station. It is a rather ambitious red terra-cotta building, with a clock in a sort of turret. Alongside it is a nondescript bicycle shop and a couple of genuine old houses. These are survivals from the country village which was here before suburbia engulfed it, but they are so covered with creepers that their character is not very plain, and one of them has a large enamel advertisement for cigarettes on its gable end. Across the road—on the right, that is to say, coming away from the church—is a pillared gateway, flanked by posts and chains, leading to a mansion designed by a pupil of Norman Shaw. This has recently been taken over as Council Offices.

If we took any of the turnings on the left, the one with the Fire

Station at the corner or one of two or three beyond it, we would find ourselves among select if old-fashioned residential streets, lined with comfortable houses mostly built about the same time as the Fire Station; solidly built, too, standing each embosked in its own shrubbery, with a conservatory attached, with its brick or rough-cast walls covered with creeper, its slate roof crowned by an ornamental ridge, and set about with well-grown trees, the clear green of acacia and sycamore, sombre evergreens, the rich copper foliage of a variegated maple, and occasionally a bushy chestnut or a prunus in delicate flower.

But we have already warned ourselves against imagining that the enticements of these mature suburban vintages comprise the whole charm of suburbia itself. The pilgrim must withstand the lures of luxuriant greenery on the one hand and period nostalgia on the other if he wants to try out his disinterestedness against suburbia unadorned. His consolation, it may be added, if he does not find all he hopes for, is that lavish adornment is an essential part of the ideal that all suburbs are striving after. But for the present the simpler if less finished picture is the more instructive.

So toiling manfully up the hill, while schoolchildren come whizzing down on bicycles, we turn eventually to the right, making for a newer residential area whose streets were only carved after the 1914 war out of the first slopes of the chalk hills in the shelter of which the original village stood. Now there is quite a colony of trim red-roofed houses, mostly semi-detached, spread out between the top of the hill and the new Cottage Hospital.

Our first impression as we penetrate the complicated pattern of curving streets in which these houses are laid out is one of surprising openness. Vegetation seems scanty, and the silhouettes of roofs and chimneys have an uncompromising look because they are not broken by the rotundity and transparency of trees. We notice the extent of the sky and contrast it with the closed-in character of the residential avenues near the bottom of the hill, up which we took a glimpse when we halted opposite the Fire Station. But if we look closer there are many signs that even in

the newest streets time and the cultivator instincts of the inhabitants are doing much to remedy this barrenness. Rock plants are
already mottling with green the low walls that separate the
pavements from the trim front gardens. Young trees have been
planted in circular holes at the edge of the pavement, though
some of them are so small they are still tied to poles for support.
Inside the gardens, shrubs of the same kinds that have always
been used to add colour and texture to uncompromising brick and
paintwork line the paths to the front porches and flank the garage
doors: laurustinus and the American currant, privet, berberis and
laurel. And creepers are being trained up trellises.

In these and other ways a varied landscape is being made to
emerge even from the regular pattern that municipalization has
brought to suburban house building; till in due course the pilgrim
to this province of suburbia will be confronted with a scene much
like the one we have already admired in the earlier suburbs, a
scene that is unified in the sense that the whole is greater than the
part, yet always seems to be changing as the pilgrim explores the
winding thoroughfares.

There are many other differences between the earlier suburbs
and the later ones, but mostly they are mere matters of fashion.
The name of the street for example—Chestnut Avenue perhaps,
or Priory Grove—though still embossed in capitals on an iron
plate, now stands by itself on a pair of wooden posts, like the station name on a country railway platform, instead of being fixed to
the fence of the corner house. This may be because high wooden
fences have largely disappeared. Low walls or hedges have taken
their place and the front gardens have thereby been thrown open
to the road, an effect which is enhanced by the narrow strip of
grass which in these new suburbs separates roadway and pavement, an extension, as it were, of the grass plots in the gardens
themselves. Then conservatories are less common, certainly the
ornamental kind attached to the house, although somewhere in
the garden there may be a small glasshouse, bought ready-made
for cultivating tomatoes and early chrysanthemums. Instead of

a conservatory there may be a garage, included within the sweep of the gabled front; instead of whitish lace or muslin curtains, coloured curtains of art silk or cretonne or repp falling straight instead of being looped back in any way; instead of smooth slate roofs, rosy tiles, and instead of arched wire frames for the pergola in the rose garden, rustic woodwork, stickily varnished. There is much less variety in the shapes and colours of chimney pots, and we note the partial disappearance (due, no doubt, to improved draughts in chimneys) of that fantastic assortment of metal cowls, bending, branching and revolving, that used to decorate the suburban skyline. We also note the partial disappearance of geometrical flower beds cut out of garden lawns, which used to be planted with lobelias and calceolarias if there was a gardener with time for bedding out, otherwise with a waving clump of pampas grass, and the complete disappearance of that phenomenon most characteristic of the old-fashioned house-front, the oval back of a dressing-table mirror seeming from the street almost to fill the rectangle of the bedroom window.

Let it be observed once more that it is the furnishings of the suburban scene—the stage properties, if you like, that stand around on the set—which we pick on as giving a clue to the character of the whole. The accumulation of these properties comprises the variegated landscape picture in which the architecture of individual houses is soon submerged. But our purpose just now is to come to even closer quarters with the suburban home, in order to see how suburbia surrounds itself with the taste of every age at once, how the past is always incorporated in the present. So let us enter any house at random—Deepdene, Grey Gables, Rotorua, The Hollies, Dunvegan, Holmlea, Bowness, The Croft, Greenways or St. Helier—reflecting as we wait for the door-bell to be answered how well these names suit the instincts and aspirations that we have already noted in the suburban resident. In them he asserts his individuality, but he also shows, in common with his next-door neighbour on either side, his leanings towards rural make-believe, and the strength as well as the romanticism of his topographical loyalties (hence the recurring flavour of Sir Walter Scott) which goes with his attachment to the squirearchical tradition.

We shall be shown straight into the drawing room. This is not the stiff front parlour, seldom sat in, of the superior artisan's house, but the family sitting room on the garden side of the house, with french windows through which the children come and go while their mothers gossip round the tea-table. The former kind of room—the ceremonial front parlour—is probably to be found in the suburb too; indeed it could be made to serve as another illustration of the suburb's use of architecture as a symbol of social standing which we noted earlier. But it is not peculiar to the suburb. It is more typical of the Victorian formality that survives best in the country town. The middle-class drawing room into which we have found our way is the essence of suburbia itself. It plays a full part in the family ritual of the fairly prosperous suburban resident. Nevertheless it has a character difficult to take in at a glance because, as with the suburb generally, its informality represents in fact an elaborate balance of forces, producing a picture in which the relationship of the part to the whole is only apparent after careful analysis.

Although, except in the mornings, it is a centre of family activities—even more so than its country-house prototype, which belongs chiefly to the female members of the family—it is as trim and well-tended as the garden outside its windows. Things are not allowed to be left lying about. Unlike the token piano in the unused parlour, the piano here is played on, if only by children practising 'The Merry Peasant', but it is still an upright, not a grand.

The room is furnished for comfort rather than ceremony, and is the one room in the house always adorned with flowers, yet it is also the place where possessions of value—or believed to be of value—are displayed: an original water colour signed by an R.A., in a frame with a gilt mount (probably a wedding present), a piece of Chelsea china, a large brass mantelpiece clock, classical in design with green marble pillars at the corners and an engraved plate telling that it was presented to the owner by his colleagues of twenty years standing as a token of their esteem. There is an elegant cabinet or bureau in Sheraton style, but comfort, on the other hand, has moulded the rather indeterminate shapes of the sofa and the two or three upholstered chairs. These have loose cretonne covers with pleated skirts. The dog is always being turned off their cushions, but not, for some reason, the cat, except as a gesture of hospitality to visitors. There are a number of small tables about: one by the sofa with current library novels and, on a lower shelf, an accumulating pile of back numbers of *Punch*, which are being kept with the idea of one day getting them bound; one, on which the radio stands, by the wall, and a folding one which is brought out at tea-time to support the Benares brass tray which the maid finds it such a burden to polish.

Paintwork is cream coloured. So is the wall-paper, but with a silver stripe. Light comes from a veined alabaster bowl hanging on a triple chain from the centre of the ceiling, and from several plated candlesticks or pottery jars converted into reading lamps which stand on the mantelpiece or the top of the piano. The floor has a patterned carpet as well as a hearth rug, and the windows have full-length curtains of a sober floral pattern. These are hung on large brass rings, threaded on a brass pole with a knob at either end, and the peculiar rasping noise they make when they are being drawn is, on a winter afternoon, as clear an indication that Sunday tea is ready as the sounding of the gong in the hall.

The room is pretty—even elegant in its own way—and sweet smelling, especially when garden scents come floating in through the open windows, but enough has been said about its furnishing to show that its charms bear no relation to the charms purveyed by the interior decorator. They are not the result of conscious discrimination between what is considered good or bad, neither do they represent the taste of any one season, or even of one generation. As in the street outside, the variety of detail determines the character of the room and proves at the same time the heterogeneous nature of suburban taste, founded on the accumulated trivia of years: on the mantelpiece, some pieces of Goss china and a row of ebony elephants in diminishing sizes; on the wall opposite, an Arundel print, a gift from an old friend of the family, and a birdscape by Peter Scott; elsewhere, a small antique table bought at a sale in a moment of extravagance, and other items that may be legacies, or fixtures taken over from the previous tenant or souvenirs of holidays abroad.

These are valued for the reasons implicit in their origin, reasons of sentiment, association, social prestige and family loyalty, and because, by surrounding himself with property of this personal kind, the suburban resident asserts his individuality in a world in which whatever is peculiar to the individual easily becomes submerged. It is sometimes said that in his domestic existence man is a slave to his furniture, that his life seems to be lived according to a ritual laid down by his obligations to his own possessions, the ritual of the tea-table, the radio set, the mowing machine, the smoker's companion and the dog that must be taken for a walk. But in the suburb he is a willing slave, enjoying the one benefit of slavery, that it spares its victims from being burdened by the uncertainties of other worlds besides the one they know. Moreover this very ritual is inseparable from the suburban environment, of which suburban man is himself the originator.

We have followed the suburban resident not only to his very doorstep but into his home, and there, at the focus of all his aspirations, we have found the same characteristics that we noticed on first penetrating into the suburban jungle, the same contrast between careful grooming and an apparently anarchical profusion of detail, and the same submission of each part to the scenic effect of the whole. But it was clear from the beginning that the suburban style is all one, indoors and out.

5

The Voice of the School Teacher

It is impossible to get away from the question of taste. We have seen that the appeal his environment makes to the man in the suburban street is not based on any of the architectural values by means of which people of taste discriminate between good and bad. Nevertheless these same people persist in condemning the suburbs because they do not conform to their own standards.

It is true that many modern suburbs are not all they might be—some, indeed, are frankly hideous—and let us not hesitate to condemn them for being so. But that is a different thing from condemning the suburbs for failing to achieve a kind of 'good' taste they never aimed at. The unworthy suburb is surely one that does not do the thing it set out to do well enough. That thing has been discussed in the foregoing chapters in relation to the place of fantasy and make-believe in everyday life, and the need for an outlet for the creative instincts of the frustrated individual. The moral, in fact, of these chapters is that the alleged 'badness' of suburban taste is not that people who live in suburbs have an unaccountable preference for what is ugly, in spite of the fact that well meant efforts to educate them into preferring more refined standards of design seem mostly based on an assumption that this is so. The people of the suburbs like their own things for their own reasons, in the light of which reasons there is much virtue in them.

Among the well meant efforts just referred to are those of various organizations which aim at improving standards of design in everyday life. Much of the everyday life with which they are concerned takes place within the suburban environment, where their scales of values is altogether a foreign one. But from their

superior station they only see the suburban villa vulgarly aping its betters in every fold and furrow of Metroland and indulging in all sorts of sentimental excesses. They feel, it seems, that if they could but begin by substituting, say, a neat neo-Georgian villa, in a more restrained taste, for those spec-builders' 'Tudorbethan' extravagances, something would already have been achieved. The brickwork of the walls would be solid though unassuming where sham half-timber work now flaunts its manorial make-believe, the panelled front door, painted a tasteful green, spick and span beneath a modest entablature, would put the flimsy pretensions of a gabled porch to shame. And with restrained Georgian go such improvements in taste as striped wallpaper in place of bouquets of gaudy flowers and limed oak furniture with wooden bars for handles in place of the veneering and graining, adorned with brass or china knobs, which a more enlightened generation can perhaps, the well-meaning people hope, be persuaded to relegate to the attic or junk shop.

As they look along the path on which they are confident that, after such a beginning, suburbia's footsteps would now be firmly set, people who mind about design see no end to the perspective of steadily improving taste. From the genteel conservatism of restrained Georgian they envisage further progress, by way of neo-Swedish or whatever similar style is currently approved as combining charm with up-to-dateness, towards a 'modern' architecture which, by gradually dispensing with the already discreet period characteristics, would become so negative in style that no one could any longer accuse it of resting on the laurels of a bygone age.

They thus associate progress with the elimination of vulgar pretentiousness. But that is not the way to reach the millennium. Leaving aside the misunderstanding it shows of the nature of modern architecture, the point is that people in suburbs are not interested in earning praise from art critics for taste that is not their own. Even if these efforts achieve some degree of success, they will not provide a stepping stone to better things. They will, instead, erect a new barrier, the barrier of snobbery of taste, between what is naturally liked now—the nearest approach we possess to a vernacular style—and the universal vernacular that all agree to be ultimately desirable. And one day, if the school-teachers are too successful, there may be no natural liking left, even of the vulgar suburban kind, but only a genteel respect for what people have been persuaded it is in the best taste to prefer.

It will be argued that style has always been imposed from above, and that even the envied vernacular of the eighteenth century was derived from fashions set by people of taste at the top of the social hierarchy, fashions accepted without question because they percolated down through society from the select few who knew what was what. But the eighteenth century, although its vernacular style is the one most present to our eyes, since it has left its mark most strongly on the English scene, is socially so far removed from the present that the comparison is hardly relevant. In those days each order of society was still accustomed to take its cue from the order above. The method by which style was disseminated was through the existing building crafts. The builder used the pattern books which recorded the London fashions to give style to his own productions, but only as and when he could adapt them to local craftsmanship methods. The process was not one that involved the ordinary man in a conscious choice, since industry had not yet confronted him with several ready-made alternatives. He merely conformed to the only taste offered him because to do so was his instinct, the whole process being part of the pattern of the settled world he belonged to.

But more significant than this is the fact that in the eighteenth century the people who set the fashions were also the leaders of the nation. The men of taste were also the men of power. Whereas today the men of taste, those whose efforts to improve the design of everyday things have already been referred to, are in general people outside the main stream of our national life. And today's men of power—the business executive, the senior civil servant, the city councillor, and the trade union leader—seldom concern themselves with such matters. Their taste, indeed, is not far removed from the taste of the suburbs. It is probable that many of them actually live there, and in the case of the rest similar impulses seem to produce similar results. A business man's residential district, like Edgbaston or Wimbledon Common, is only suburbia writ large, and in the more exclusive parts of the Chilterns and in the stockbroking country round East Grinstead and Haywards Heath the pilgrim who has visited suburbia will find much that has a familiar look. The same red-tiled roof peaks peer romantically from surrounding trees, though their hips and valleys have been modelled, and the tone of their rustic tiles selected, by an expensive architect. The same well-polished furniture fills the lounge hall, reflecting the coloured light from the heraldic glass in the staircase window, though in these houses some of the pieces may be genuine antiques. The same well-tended lawns are enclosed by the same hedges and flowering shrubs, though several gardeners may be employed to do the pruning and clipping and mowing. Here, in fact, in the flesh, is the suburban dream come true, but the owners of these dream establishments do not regard themselves as the arbiters of anybody's taste. And from these strongholds of opulence and influence the people who know what is good find themselves shouldered out by people who know what they like.

To say that you know what you like is usually to imply contempt for what people with more authority say you ought to like. It is the philistine's declaration of independence. But today's men of power are at least realists when they take this line, because they understand instinctively that their power is not expressed, as power was in the eighteenth century, by ability to impose a visible pattern on the society they govern. In those days the visible pattern—the standard of design—created by those at the top permeated society to the bottom because it was accepted as a mark of authority as well as a criterion of culture and good breeding. Now it is only a fad. Good design has lost its power as an influence since it no longer stands for anything outside itself.

If it is agreed that, in its role as an architectural vernacular of sorts, the suburb must have a firm foundation on what ordinary people like and are themselves willing to help to create, the question may still perhaps be asked whether people do, in fact, like the style of architecture we have labelled the suburban style, or are we falsely crediting it with representing popular contemporary taste? It is claimed by some that the suburban resident is not really a free agent and that his choice is limited by his ignorance of the alternatives, or even that he is given no choice at all. Is it really the case, however, that an innocent and unwilling public is made to accept whatever villainies the speculative builder chooses to force upon him? The speculative builder can no doubt be blamed for much, but he is a business man supplying a demand and, as business men must, he instinctively reacts to the nature of the demand. It is true that his reaction is slow and that his attachment to what has proved popular before perpetuates a tradition that might otherwise change more quickly, but this is in keeping with all vernacular architecture, which comes to identify itself with the society it caters for by a gradual process of like breeding like, until there is no question of alternative styles and no one can say to whom blame or credit should be given, or whether the builder builds what he knows is wanted or the public wants what it is accustomed to see built.

All evidence goes to show that when the public is given a choice, the kind of architecture it chooses is very like that which it is already being given. There is no popular demand for what superior people call 'good taste'. Many local planning acts contain a so-called 'amenities clause' which allows the local council to control new building on aesthetic grounds as well as on grounds of structure, sanitation and the like, and the way this clause usually operates is instructive. Plans for all proposed houses must be passed by a special committee appointed by the council. This committee is composed of ordinary people—councillors and their kind—and what usually happens is that it approves without question all designs for what it regards as ordinary houses, but it rejects the freaks out of hand. Often the 'freaks' turn out to be houses specially designed by architects, which stand out clearly from the ordinary builder's output, and the architect complains because it seems to him that he, a qualified designer, is being taught his business by a group of mere public officials.

His attitude is understandable, and he has a right to complain, especially when only he and his client are concerned with an isolated site that happens to come within the council's boundaries. But if, as sometimes happens, the house in question forms part of a suburban community—and it is particularly in the fast-growing suburbs that these amenity clauses are thought to be most required—then the local councillor may well be following right instincts if he rejects an architect's design, a design exhibiting the mannerisms of consciously advanced taste, on account of its strangeness. He is speaking with the voice of the people he officially represents, and he knows instinctively that this unfamiliar animal is not among the fauna indigenous to the country he rules over. It has wandered in by mistake, and its continued presence would only destroy the spell under which the suburban magic operates. His decision is not a reflection on the architect's competence as a designer, for the councillor knows nothing about art. He knows what people like.

What people like, however, as we have seen, is closely bound up with what people ask of their environment, and how many new ideas they are ready to admit into it. We found that to draw a parallel with the eighteenth century was rather misleading, since a peculiar combination of circumstances enabled it to produce a style of design that was autocratic and at the same time popular, and no conflict resulted from the spread of new ideas. Contemporary circumstances are different. We may perhaps learn more about popular taste in a contemporary setting by looking for a moment at another land instead of another century—at the experience of Russia between the two wars—though in going so far afield we shall be seeking guidance from a world that is in most respects as remote from suburbia as the moon.

The new world the Soviet Union created in 1917 launched itself at once into a series of exciting experiments, architectural ones among them. It was a period of enthusiasm for whatever was new, when anything that related to the old regime was willingly discarded. The revolutionary architecture of Europe—represented by those attempts at founding a non-historical style on the geometrical basis of steel and concrete construction, which various pioneers had so bravely initiated in the early years of the century—was conveniently at hand. What could be more natural than for Moscow to act as foster mother to a movement so much in keeping with her iconoclastic impulses and so clearly suited to the new world of which she was now the centre?

Enthusiastically but seriously Russia adopted the new architecture as her own; she invited no less a person than M. le Corbusier to come and advise her; with his help and that of other experts from outside, as well as her own architectural *avant-garde*, she put up boldly modern buildings in the shape of workers' flats, trade union clubs, co-operative stores. Conscientiously her parks of rest and culture showed that they disowned the academic prettifications with which the bourgeois world had deceived itself for so long. But what has become of this uncompromising modernism now? Columns and pediments are back again, but not, as some are only too eager to maintain, because the Soviet Union is no longer revolutionary or because modern architecture was a fad that did not last. Admittedly the quality of some of the new buildings was faulty, because they represented a style of architecture belonging to an industrial age, and therefore needing a highly technical, industrialized building industry to support it, which Russia did not possess. But may not the real reason for the change be that the Russians are realists and knew that their revolutionary architecture was in danger of becoming too artificial by out-running public preparedness for it?

In a country in which a public sense of participation in the national well-being is essential to successful growth, architecture, like many other things, must be made to serve as an expression of corporate ideals, and must remain within the orbit of public understanding. What the mass of the Russian public—like the mass of English suburban residents—require of their architecture is a sense that it represents what they themselves are striving after, and it must do so in a language they already understand. You cannot use architecture as a symbol of anything, if you leave out the very features that constitute the alphabet of symbolism. Columns and cornices, to the man in the Russian street, served as a reassuring demonstration of solidity and permanence in a world that in many other respects was shaking the very ground under his feet, and he was thankful to accept them as proof of the stability of the new regime in the same way that he accepted the showmanship of the monster parades that periodically crowded the vast pavements of the Red Square. He was not yet prepared to interest himself in the intellectual satisfaction to be obtained from eliminating the inessentials of architecture to the point of pure geometry or in the aesthetic imagination that inspired the *esprit nouveau.*

In fact for all their distance apart, geographically and spiritually, Moscow and Metroland have this in common, that architecture is to them not an art form to be accepted or rejected according to the rules of aesthetic taste. It is a symbol of what is real and tangible in an uncertain world, contributing to their environment the comforts of familiarity. They both listen with respect to the superior persons who tell them what is best in contemporary design and what they will therefore get most credit by preferring, but the voice of the school-teacher is powerless against the instinct for self-preservation. Nothing is to be gained, the instinct of the suburban resident tells him, by condemning the make-believe of spec-builder's Tudor when the thing that is most valued about it is its cosiness and familiarity, which makes it a secure anchorage in a changeable world. Nothing is to be gained by criticizing the academic heaviness or the clumsy detail of the Moscow Metro when the thing that is most valued about it is that its walls are lined with expensive marbles which in a pre-revolutionary world would have adorned a prince's banqueting hall. It is real and solid, suggesting a prosperity that has come to stay.

The lesson to be learnt from Russia of the 'twenties and 'thirties, therefore, is that it is no use trying to impose a strange new style on any public, since architecture will lose its meaning for the public if it changes faster than the popular demand for it. Other kinds of progress, economic and educational, may be necessary before what the outside observer means by architectural progress can even begin. A few pages back, when referring to the difference between the eighteenth century and now, from the point of view of the significance that can be attached to standards of taste, I said that design had lost its authority because it no longer stands for anything outside itself. One would like to say to the people who preach the virtues of good design: these virtues will not be popularly recognized until they are associated once again with other standards and have become symbolic of other qualities.

The complaint is often made that the man in the street is apathetic about planning and design. Perhaps this is partly the caution of conservatism; he feels he cannot be sure whether what planning offers him has enough in common with what he likes about the unplanned world he knows. But evidence shows that he will accept what is generally meant by good design quickly enough when it is identified—as once it used to be—with the things he requires the physical world to provide for him. As things are, he is following sound instincts in refusing to welcome modern design in all its purity and discipline. If he did so he would be entering a fool's paradise, since he would only find himself enjoying the shadow of the modern world without its substance—the substance being, of course, its economic benefits. All agree on the need for a new vernacular, but the best means of bringing architecture back to serving popular needs are not necessarily architectural means.

All this may seem to be leading to the somewhat defeatist suggestion that we can do nothing but wallow in architectural anarchy until the economic benefits of the modern world have been extended to all its inhabitants, freeing them from the need of the protective embrace of a familiar environment and enabling them to welcome a new age unreservedly, together with all the arts that belong to it. But the issue is not as simple as that. In the contemporary world generally, architecture has its place as one of the weapons of progress. Although it is true that in this country modern design has shown a tendency to get out of touch with the mass of society it serves, and for various reasons which we cannot go into here—such as the increased use of synthetic materials—to develop a style beyond ordinary people's understanding, it is on the whole identified with good planning and with the idea of architecture being made to serve the community. And architecture can itself fulfil the purpose of advertising the potential of the modern world. It can show people what science ought to be able to do for them, and therefore it has in its nature the germ of a solution to the very problem we have just been discussing.

But this is not a book about the role of architecture in the modern world. It is about its place in the modern suburb—or, rather, with the whole suburban environment, in which architecture in the narrow sense plays but a secondary part. The suburban world, as I have been at pains to point out, is not to be taken as a cross-section of the general world, whose problems are largely those created by the transitional stage through which it is passing. The suburb is a peculiar self-contained phenomenon with its own needs and impulses, and whatever the eventual development of architecture in general, the very reasons for the suburb's existence demand that the suburban style shall continue to contain an element of fantasy and make-believe. It may even tend to differentiate itself more, as time goes on, from the planned world outside, by stressing its anarchical character and its preoccupation with the whim of the individual. In any case, should it not be approached with the sympathy it deserves on account of the frequent misrepresentation of its true nature?

Should not the bad suburbs be condemned only for doing badly what it is their business to do? Should not criticism help the badly built and badly planned suburbs to be better built and better planned, and above all, recognizing their value as an outlet for fantasy, should not it help them to become a better outlet for more fantasy? To inculcate restraint and refinement—which are admirable qualities to set off a life lived at full stretch in the bustle of the busy world—in the depth of the suburban jungle is only to put a brake on the creative instinct and therefore on the proper exercise of some of its most valuable functions. This is illustrated in the 'improved' suburb, the model garden city, where the very virtues the enthusiasts claim for it are in fact its defects. By careful planning and controlled good taste they have eliminated the very qualities of romance and rhetoric on which the suburban style flourishes.

These garden cities can also claim that they set a high standard of layout and the provision of public services. Such matters are of course the proper province of the expert, and can safely be placed in his care. But in matters of the eye it is safe to say that in the modern world design tends to become too professionalized. It has become the exclusive province of the expert, and further support is given to our claim that the suburban style represents— for better or worse—the nearest approach to a contemporary vernacular by the fact that the suburb is the one hide-out of the amateur, on whose participation a living tradition must always depend.

To take an illustration from another art, the English water-colour tradition, which we admire in the work of a few outstanding painters, was really founded on the unpretending enthusiasm of the talented amateur. The genius of these few would never have come to fruition if it had not been for the generations of Englishmen and Englishwomen sketching away happily during their vacations, filling portfolios with tender reminiscences of English topography and covering their drawing room walls with representations of Alps and Lakes and Trossachs. At one time the ability to paint in water colours was part of every gentleman's equipment, and even now it is an art that thrives on account of the number of people who enjoy practising it for its own sake. Similarly, the picturesque tradition represented by the

English suburban scene is preserved by the enthusiastic if somewhat inexpert efforts of the amateur. Owing to the expense of building as a hobby, the amateur architect is rare, although at one time he had a good deal to do with the founding of the villa tradition which the suburban style has adopted as its own. The country squire who amused himself with Gothic gate lodges would find it hard, perhaps, to recognize his progeny; still more so the proud proprietor of a *cottage ornée* in the style of Batty Langley and the industrious landscapist with his clumps and his *coups d'oeil*. Nevertheless, the connection is there. The hamlet at Blaise Castle, which I mentioned in Chapter Two, was a prototype in more senses than one. But if not with amateur architects, the present-day suburb is peopled with amateur gardeners, amateur landscapists and amateur decorators, with contrivers of all sorts of effects, with handymen and with the individualists from whom the suburban jungle draws much of its vitality and for whose creative instincts it caters in a way that nothing else can as the world is made at present.

The suburb can only be sympathetically viewed in relation to the lives and interests of such people. The suburban style is not a style of architecture but the setting of suburban life itself, and its 'taste' is but the local colour the inhabitants gather round themselves in accordance with their peculiar instincts and aspirations. If you take this colour away by teaching them that there are other tastes they ought to prefer, or by means of any other improvements imposed from without, you take away suburbia itself.

6

The Origin of the Species

Suburbia is not, as the literal meaning of the word suggests, solely a geographical term, although it happens that, for very good reasons, suburbs have generally grown on the fringes of towns. It is a term for the environment created by and for one class of people to suit their special needs. It is not therefore sufficient to refer to the inhabitants of the suburbs as 'they', as though they were something inexplicable in a menagerie. If we want to learn more about the peculiar nature of the suburbs, we must try to find out who these people are and what they have in common to bring them together. The question we must ask is: how can the people who make up the suburban population be distinguished from the rest of society?

The distinction is not one of income, nor is it one of social class—the age-old distinction between gentle and simple has little meaning here. Nevertheless, since English society still tends to be stratified according to both these classifications, we are bound to find them in evidence in any congregation of people, whatever its origin, and it is fairly true to say—though this is not the only significant thing about them—that the suburbs are peopled from the middle and lower middle class. These terms must be used in the broadest sense, because they must be understood to include people ranging in occupation from the stockbroker to the artisan. The range, it may be noted, has broadened greatly in recent times. In fact one of the characteristic phenomena of our generation is the growing availability of the suburbs to lower income groups—not, as some enthusiasts would have us believe, because to build in the form of suburbs is intrinsically better than to build in any other way, but because of the tendency for that element in society by and for whom suburbs are produced to occur at increasingly various income levels.

This is what allows us to study the suburb as a development within the main stream of English life, not as a mere period phenomenon. The first suburbs were essentially upper middle class. They began as the villas of the prosperous merchants and near gentry, who came spanking into the City from Highgate behind their smart cobs or indulged their wives and families with the luxury of a rural retreat at Richmond or Strand-on-the-Green. Later, with the coming of mechanical transport, a suburban life became the privilege of the less opulent middle class, and the Norwoods and Balhams, the Lewishams and Cricklewoods, became the promised land of the black-coated thousands who formed the backbone of English commercial life. After them came poorer people still, many of whom had previously been crowded together into slums. Now they found themselves decanted from their grimy bye-law streets into garden suburbs and new speculative estates, following the spread of cheap public transport and the change of housing policy on the part of municipal bodies from one that favoured tenements to one that favoured decentralized housing estates. The sociabilities of the shared lawn mower and the suburban bowling club gradually replaced the Cockney jovialities of the Mile End Road.

But this migration to suburbia is not solely the result of the provision of public transport and the pursuit of health and unpolluted air. It is the result of the increase in numbers and influence of the particular element in society of which I have already spoken, and which can be said to have invented suburban life as its own appropriate environment. What, we must ask again, is the nature of this element, since it has neither a class nor income basis—yet contains a limited range of both? How has it come to develop so actively in recent years that its characteristic style of environment can now almost be said to dominate twentieth-century England?

This is not an easy question to answer, but I suggest that we can best begin by looking at the suburban world in relation to the part its inhabitants play in the world as a whole. Even at the risk of rising too far above the cosy labyrinth of streets and shrubberies and porches and perambulator sheds into which our voyages of exploration have hitherto taken us, and losing ourselves in the windy uplands of sociological theory, let us look at the suburban world for the time being as part of a complex organism called human society which nevertheless functions according to certain scientific laws. The people who are accustomed to look at the world in this way are the economists, and it may be useful to adopt some of their jargon.

The economists are concerned with how society functions, and they describe its machinery as consisting of three elements. These are summarized by three words which are not the less fundamental for having long ago become clichés: production, consumption, and distribution. These represent, respectively, the elementary process of supply and demand and the means by which it operates. All human activities, moreover, can be related to one or other of these fundamentals; these three terms, that is to say, can also be used to differentiate three kinds of work. The picture, however, must not be over simplified, since few human activities are related exclusively to one of these fundamentals. It is more likely that any activity we choose to consider will be found to be related to all three simultaneously (in fact it is almost necessary that this should be so if society is to function at all), but there is generally to be found a *bias* in favour of one.

The economist thus draws our attention to an already existing classification of quite a different kind from those associated with class and income and other conventional groupings. But his is not so much a classification of people, as a classification of the kinds of life or culture to which they owe allegiance, according to the part they play in the society they belong to. It is therefore also a classification of the direction in which they seek fulfilment for themselves.

One way in which people seek fulfilment is through the environment they provide for themselves, and it is worth considering whether a direct physical equivalent does not exist, in the shape of a characteristic environment, for at least two of the economist's three categories. To begin with production: production depends primarily on the land. When one speaks of the land, one perhaps evokes in some people's eyes a picture of an old-fashioned world based on handicraft, but in the sense that is intended here the activities that belong to the land include up-to-date scientific ones as well as the oldest ones of all, blast furnaces and hydro-electric undertakings as well as the yearly ritual of harvest-home. Perhaps a better word than land would be region. From the land all wealth originates, but it originates in different forms according to regional differences of climate, geological structure and so on. Can we not say, therefore, that production can be identified with activities which are largely regional, and can we not also say that the *city* can be identified with consumption, since it exists to turn the products of the regions to the benefit of society collectively?

To put it another way, production and consumption seem generally to correspond to the physical realities, country and town. The producing element in society has always exercised its function by a process of decentralization; individual members of the community have forced themselves away from their fellows into the open spaces to dig its products out of the land. Similarly the consuming element is synonymous with centralization. The city is an expression of the herding instinct, one that acts automatically because man is, in one of his aspects, a gregarious animal. He does not, in the first place, herd with his fellows in order to find a means of subsistence; he seeks a means of subsistence in order to be able to find his fulfilment with the herd; that is, for consumption rather than production—consumption of company, beer, cinemas, friendship and all the stimuli that arise from association with others of his kind.

The conclusion these speculations lead to is that, in their basic meaning, town and country (or the city and the region) are not different degrees of the same thing. They are different in *kind*, though complementary in the sense of being each necessary to the other. They are the physical expression of opposing types of culture, urbanism tending to be international in character and regionalism to be differentiative, the culture of place. It would be outside the purpose of this book to explore this distinction further, in order to see what light it throws on contemporary problems; whether, for example, it helps to explain the unsatisfactory nature of our large industrial towns by showing that they are not by rights towns at all in the sense of originating in the gregarious instincts of the consumer. Is it not more natural for industry (being a productive activity) to be regional—as indeed it has been at other moments in its history—and are not our so-called industrial cities merely a transitory grouping of producers round coal and iron deposits, a grouping that electric power and other new developments are perhaps already in the process of liquidating?

It is relevant to our present purpose, however, to suggest that —in so far as one can generalize about such things—those who seek their fulfilment in production find it in non-urban life, and those who seek it in consumption find it in non-rural life. But there is still the economist's third category to be considered. Where can those who seek fulfilment in the distributive activities— the ubiquitous commercial population, for example, of an increasingly commercial world—hope to find it? Unhappily, the answer must be that with the exception of one positive achievement, they have been largely frustrated in their attempts to create for themselves a setting that will satisfy their peculiar needs and aspirations, and their abortive efforts to do so lie scattered up and down the country, producing much of the chaos we complain about today. If we examine the places where this chaos is most in evidence we shall find that they all relate to distribution in one shape or another, to the unassimilated world of modern commerce: the village street that has become a car park, the ribbon development along the arterial road, and the road houses and petrol stations that have blossomed there. The exception I speak of is the new world of the suburb, whose growth has coincided so exactly with the growth in complexity of distribution itself. All the evidence, in fact, indicates that the middle-men, and the others who owe allegiance to the world of distribution, represent that very element in society to which I referred at the beginning of this chapter as responsible for creating the suburb.

Before we go further with identifying the leafy recesses of the suburban world with the aspirations of those who operate this distribution machinery, we must examine the nature of the machinery more closely. Production and the consumer have always, of course, been linked by (and dependent on) some sort of distribution machinery, and in earlier times the way it functioned was relatively simple. The farmer took his own goods to market, and the housewife bought from him direct. The market place—which came a little later—did not threaten the amenities of town or country, and even when the process became more complex it only had the effect of inserting an extra cog-wheel into the machinery of existence; the merchant and the moneylender growing fat on the increasing separation of the town consumer from direct contact with the country producer.

But the past two hundred years or so have seen a remarkable growth in the complexity of the distribution technique, and therefore in the influence it has exerted over the social pattern. Ever since the producer ceased to be self-sufficient, but became a consumer of other people's products besides his own—ever since, for example, the countryman ceased to make his own furniture and weave his own cloth—this process has been steadily accelerating. It has always been the case that at different times in history different elements have dominated the social scene. For many generations, in particular, problems of production were constantly to the fore, and the current type of civilization was a producer civilization. Today the world is dominated by problems of distribution; so much so that it can almost be said that these are the typical unsolved problems of the modern world.

We adopted the label 'distribution' ready-made when we took over the abstract but elementary jargon of the economist. But it can be a misleading term, suggesting only the distribution of

goods, whereas the impact of the new complexity of distribution technique, though coinciding with the growth of trade,
is a phenomenon of much wider significance. Translated into
physical terms, the abstraction, distribution, becomes the function,
communication; and not only in the literal sense of transport and
travel facilities, but in the complete sense of the contacts a community maintains between its different parts. This is, of course, the
sense in which economists have always used the word.

The growth in the importance of communications and all that
they have brought in their train, and their disturbing impact on
the tidy pattern that belonged to the old days when town was
town and country was country, is thus synonymous with the growth
of the necessity for highly specialized planning. For planning is—
and always has been—nothing but a method of ensuring that, in
spite of the new complexity of their relations, the machinery that
correlates the two worlds of production and consumption works as
smoothly as may be.

To find an illuminating example of the impact just referred to,
we need look no further than that same market town which we
have already mentioned. The market town began as a revolutionary enterprise, since it brought about the downfall of the feudal
manor, its predecessor as a distribution centre. But it was so simple
and natural that it took its place easily in the old social complex,
without at first introducing new problems. For a time the English
town still remained a logical and satisfactory affair, but when
improved travel facilities brought the individual market town into
the web of the national transport pattern, its nuclear shape became obsolete. As typical of the eighteenth century as the market
town was of an earlier system, is the ribbon town (or coaching
town) consisting of the old village high street magnified into a built-
up section of a post road, its central culminating point being the
coaching inn, the stopping place of the coaches which gave this new
type of town its importance to the world outside. This ribbon town
of the eighteenth century is a typical English phenomenon; Coln-
brook, Marlborough, Thame, Reigate, the pattern is ubiquitous.

Topographers speak of towns like these with affection, and many of them do possess the grace and charm we associate with Georgian building. But in spite of the pictorial appeal of the regular sequence of Georgian façades, of the enhanced charm of individual taste when it flourishes within the disciplined framework of a consistent idiom, and of its sense of civic unity, the fact remains that the eighteenth-century ribbon town is not an urban development at all. To call it so is, in fact, another example of our habit of identifying and confusing the idea of urbanism with any concentration of bricks and mortar, as in the case of the nineteenth-century manufacturing town. The Georgian coaching town is but an early instance of the ribbon development that later, with the further growth of the influence of distribution, was allowed to ruin the shapeliness of town and countryside. It must therefore be acknowledged that, in spite of Georgian architecture's high reputation, the English have not built good towns since they were first confronted with the problem of adjusting themselves to this disrupting influence. From the planning point of view Georgian towns seldom got beyond the primitive stage of automatic response to external stimuli, with the exception of a few places like Bath (which was of course nothing but an outpost of the consumer's metropolis) and a few residential quarters inside other towns.

But if the English did not make good towns they invented the suburb. In general only chaos has resulted from the impact of the new distribution techniques, and only planning can repair it, planning being, as we have seen, the technique of making such adjustments smoothly. But when the new techniques—or, rather, the communities that owe their way of life to them—have been allowed to start from scratch and devise unhindered a new kind of environment suited to their nature, they have achieved something that provides at least a partial answer to the unfulfilled aspirations of their peculiar world.

In the suburbs, as well as strung out untidily along the arterial roads, are the homes of the middlemen, who are not true town dwellers because they do not congregate in towns as a result of their gregarious instincts, or their belief in the unifying principle. On the contrary, they dislike town life and are always pursuing a make-believe country life. They would, however, equally detest real country life. They only sat themselves down where they did because there was no place for them in a society that was changing more quickly than its physical framework was prepared for, except the fringes of the population they depended on. These outlying districts, the village market place turned by circumstances into one section of an arterial road, can be said to exemplify in a single picture both the increase in significance of distribution as an activity, and the chaos that has resulted from the way of life that derives from it not being properly catered for.

In the suburb, on the other hand, the man who owes allegiance to this way of life has built for himself a congenial home. His distribution activities, by their very nature, take place here, there and everywhere, but the suburb is the place where he has put down his roots, the only place where he is not an outcast, not the odd man out, spoiling the tidy pattern of a traditional countryside. It is not surprising, therefore, that he clings loyally to the suburban idea, in the face of the contempt of metropolitan man for everything suburbia stands for. This contempt is, of course, simply an expression of the conflict between the man whose ideals are attainable through consumer activities and the man whose ideals are attainable through distributor activities, but it has been aggravated by the fact that the former is the more articulate—the town planners and sociological theorists come from his ranks—whereas we can only appreciate the potentialities of the suburbs if we discard the consumer prejudices of the city intellectual and look at them from the point of view of the distributor himself.

It is not suggested that the suburbs are entirely peopled by those engaged in the distributive trades and transport and the other activities we have classed with them—it takes all sorts to make even a suburban world—only that they represent the human side of what the new complexity of distribution technique has brought to modern life. This is in fact what is generally called the middle class. I do not want to trespass on the economist's territory —still less on the social historian's—but I do not think it is too naive an interpretation of their summary of events to say that the rise of a powerful middle class coincided with distribution's rise in significance and complexity—that is, with the dominating influence of commerce. Out of the business of bringing producer and consumer together in an increasingly complex society, this new class created a world of its own and peopled it with individuals pursuing numerous new activities: the stockbroker, the tram conductor, the income-tax collector, the garage mechanic, the shorthand typist, the advertising man. Their name is legion and the job of all of them is simply to oil the distributive machinery.

Those are the people who have made the suburbs what they are, and the purpose of these rather tentative sociological speculations is simply to try and throw some light on the instincts and aspirations that we noted earlier as characteristic of suburban dwellers, by reference to their origin in the world of distribution. For it is quite impossible, if we are willing to run the risk of oversimplification, to isolate a kind of individual temperament that goes with each of the economist's classifications. There may not exist any one individual possessing exactly such a temperament, since all individuals owe allegiance to all three categories in varying proportions, but where the bias lies is reflected in the temperament.

The man with a bias towards production, for example, seeks his fulfilment in place. Throughout history his has been the mystical earth culture; his art is symbolic and romantic; his politics feudal, Tory or patriarchal. The man with a bias towards consumption, is, by contrast, gregarious. He is the townee, the intellectual and the aesthete, the Whig rather than the Tory. He prefers a life of assimilation and earns his living by the use of forms or symbols divorced (as far as the physical world allows anything to be divorced) from physical production. His art is abstract or classic. His is the unifying, as distinct from the differentiating, principle, which builds cities and civilizations and is founded on the things of the mind. Society to him means its political structure and systems, and it is he in particular who has always seen political progress as progress towards that egalitarian, international state which is the only one that can satisfy his mind's sense of oneness.

Finally, the man with a bias towards distribution is, as we have seen, quite different from the other two. He is often confused with the first, but he is an extrovert—a materialist, in contrast to the mystic whom we find at the basis of the production culture. The mystic enjoys his sport, the materialist his *sports*. The latter—the distributor—is the life-long games player, the 'hearty', who judges everything by its physical perfection, whether motor cars, film stars or his own kind, in whose good-fellowship he indulges so irrepressibly. The ball-game cult coincides with his rise into prominence, and he is the embodiment of the team spirit.

In the last chapter I mentioned that the creative instinct for which the suburb provides an outlet is essentially an individualistic one, and now we can see why. The instincts of the man belonging to the world of distribution are all towards anarchy. This applies equally to his political instincts, though these are often disguised as liberalism (or, when he is thwarted, as Fascism). His system is *laisser-faire*, his ethics enlightened self-interest and his philosophy the survival of the fittest. The so-called 'Americanization' of modern life is largely identifiable with his influence. His art is one of *pastiche*, and his architecture that of fancy dress, which gives us an additional reason why neither an enforced revival of peasant arts (which grew up in the region) nor the imposition of an academic rule of thumb (which belongs to the classical art of the metropolis) is acceptable in the suburb. Rather than condemn the suburbs for preferring period styles, we should understand that they cannot be expected to like anything at all until it has some of the attributes of a period style.

In the deep recesses of the suburban jungle, screened from the outside world, the urge towards individualism and anarchy, which is thus natural to one section of society, can safely be allowed full play, and a passion for *pastiche* can direct itself into fruitful instead of abortive channels. Uncontrolled building of the suburban kind may and does add to the general architectural chaos of our time, but the suburb itself—at its best—has virtues peculiarly designed to bring comfort and fulfilment to many. At its worst we can still say of it that its faults are not its own but arise from its association with the unassimilated products of the commercial world.

7

Compactness Above All

A legitimate complaint against suburbia is that it spreads itself too widely. As the motorist drives out of town along his concreted highway, his hopes of green fields are frustrated mile after mile. Though kerbstones give place to wide green verges and side turnings offer glimpses of gravelled country lanes, he still finds himself confined between barriers of bricks and mortar, to say nothing of the dwarf walls and garden gates, the shrubberies and rock gardens guarded by lead statuary, that form the outworks of this impenetrable fortification. And when the single ribbon of building breaks away, as it does every now and then, into deep bastions of residential development, fanning out inland until they seem to threaten the existence of rurality itself, the motorist sees with alarm a future England that has become, in effect, one enormous built-up area.

Occasionally he is made aware that the phenomenon about which he complains is not quite as new as it seems. A moss-grown wall, backed by wellingtonias and monkey puzzles, only partially conceals a slate-roofed villa from which the stucco is now peeling sadly and whose garden, seen through a rusty iron gate, is overgrown with weeds, but which was once the pride of some successful tradesman from the nearby town. A public house, which now flourishes on the passing motorist's custom as well as serving as the local for the newly populated neighbourhood, once made its profits from supplying a change of post-horses to the users of the coach road. We can deduce its previous history from the Georgian gable that appears above the new plate-glass bay window of the bar parlour, from the extent of disused stabling at the back (which the landlord is thinking of converting into a tea lounge, with the help of some potted palms and a radiogram) and finally, if we care to enter the saloon bar, from a framed engraving on the wall depicting the simple rectangular façade of the 'Coach and Horses' before the magnificence of its roughcast and terra-cotta additions made it so notable a landmark. And when the schoolchildren scamper across the highway to the annoyance of the speeding motorist, he may notice that the object of their perilous journey is a sweetshop whose wares—which also include lemonade and minerals—are displayed behind the cast iron casements of what was once the gate lodge of a Victorian gentleman's park. The lodge is of brick and flint in *cottage ornée* style. The pavement in front, which is walled with enamel advertisements for Schweppes and St. Julian Flake, has been carved out of a closely planted shrubbery, and through this a path leads to some wooden sheds at the side, on which is a notice: 'Cycle Repairs. Punctures Mended.' Behind is a belt of fir trees and on the other side of the lodge the driveway which once led into the park but now leads to a building estate with vacant plots still for sale.

Thus can we see numerous survivals of earlier sporadic building strung out across the countryside, along the highways that join town to town. It was suggested in the last chapter that only during recent times—since the technique of commerce has come to dominate our existence—has it been necessary to regard this ribbon development as a menace, instead of something that brought variety, as the gentlemen's lodges and the coaching inns did previously, to the tedium of a lengthy journey. Ribbon development, moreover, is only a particularly aggravating instance of the general spread of uncontrolled building, which is most prevalent along the highways because these lines of communication are at the same time the instruments that have facilitated the rise of the commercial world and the location where its products deposit themselves most freely.

It was also suggested that the chaos found in places like these is due to the failure of new techniques to become assimilated into the old pattern, and that the rise of the commercial world is therefore identifiable with the rise of the need for planning. The commercial world is founded on the complexity of modern distribution technique. Operating on a scale that ignores regional and local differences, its impact is inevitably of a kind that needs control. It has no pattern of its own. An analogy may perhaps be drawn between the chaos we see almost wherever we look about us, and a house in which the services—the plumbing, the drainage, the telephone and heating systems—have become so complicated that they not only festoon the outside (as indeed in modern houses they tend to do in practice) but spread out into the garden and even trip one up when one tries to enter the front door. It is as though the people in charge of these services—stokers, plumbers and telephone engineers—were constantly bustling up and down stairs, interfering in a maddening way with the normal life of the occupants. These services having been invented, the owners of the house feel bound to make use of them, and they add considerably to the comfort and convenience of life, but if the owners want to have the advantages they bring without being overwhelmed by their very presence, they must keep them in their place even to the extent of replanning the whole house round them.

This is, in effect, what the town planner's activities consist of, in places where the impact of the new on the old is too destructive to be bearable, and his right to control sporadic building up and down the arterial road is disputed by no one except a few whose profits he may cause to diminish. It is important, however, that the sporadic building that occurs on the fringes of towns should not be confused with suburbia itself, despite the fact that they have socially a common origin of the kind described in the last chapter, and therefore share the same architectural idiom. The ribbon building that spoils the motorist's view of the green fields on either side of the highway represents the commercial world—the product of new distribution techniques—totally at a loss to fit itself into the existing physical pattern, while the suburb at its best represents a new pattern which this world has created for itself. We have already seen that two of the typical characteristics of suburbia are that, far from trespassing on anyone else's world, it insists on creating a circumscribed world of its own from which all others must be shut out, and that it is a synthetic product based on nothing that existed before.

In actual practice, of course, these two phenomena, the true suburbia and the scattered fragments of suburban housing along the highways and elsewhere, merge into one another. The confusion caused thereby—and indeed the very existence of much of this scattered housing—can partly be blamed on the enthusiasm for decentralization that has so strongly influenced the building of houses in recent years. The advocates of this policy, impressed by the virtues of the suburban way of life, seem to have imagined that these virtues came from spacing buildings widely. In their horror of the overcrowded slum life that had grown up in cities, the garden suburb reformers advocated dispersal as the one essential principle and legislation to limit the number of houses that might be built on each acre of ground as the one essential measure of control. They apparently did not understand that the real cause of slums is not congestion but poverty, and they therefore never foresaw that the only result of decanting a poverty-stricken slum population into new housing estates outside the town might be to perpetuate the same conditions whilst depriving their victims of the consolation that company provides.

Though less noisome and spectacular, since their defects are social more than physical, the new slums of the outlying areas are as discreditable as those of central smoke-begrimed London. Where a dormitory estate has been deposited at random—or anywhere that land is cheap—there is no focus for the life of the community inhabiting it. Often there is not even a pub. The boredom of the housewife marooned at the end of a straggling succession of half-made roads is worse than that of the Scottish crofter in winter time. He can find fulfilment in a life of semi-isolation, but she is temperamentally dependent on the stimulus provided by social intercourse and the ready-made recreations of modern life for which her never-silent radio is but a poor substitute. Hence the popularity of the houses strung out along the arterial roads. Ribbon development is often blamed on the villainy of the speculative builder who is so cunning as to put his houses where road surfaces and sewers are to be found already in existence. But people like a bit of life, and despite the dangers of the speeding traffic, the housewife, busy at her kitchen sink, likes to see the world pass by her window.

This is all very well as a makeshift, but apart from the topographical disaster that ribbon development entails, the highway's passing show can never compensate the suburban housewife and her family for the absence of a well-rounded existence, which they will never achieve in such a situation. As we have seen, the separate world of the suburb has been specially created with this need in view. Its self-sufficiency is at the core of its character, and who could carve a homely enclave out of a foreign world—and contrive within it a self-contained landscape—if so uncompromising a reminder of the outer world's foreignness as an arterial highway tore noisily through the midst of it? The groves of the suburban jungle must be kept sacred to the suburban ritual.

The wide spacing of buildings as such therefore brings no benefit to anyone. Decentralization is not a cure for slums. It only means the substitution of one problem for another, and as a considered policy on the part of those in authority, it only represents an evasion of their responsibility for removing the causes of the poverty out of which slum conditions have arisen, and for raising the standard of city planning generally. The function of the suburb is not to remedy the defects of city life; it is to provide another kind of life for a kind of people to whom the city environment is unsuited. It may be that our bored housewife, watching the passing traffic from the scullery window or half listening to the radio as she moves from room to room, would be happier in the hum of the city, if her standard of life there were raised and if she had clean air to breathe and a playground for the children. But maybe her proper *milieu* is suburbia, with its offering of a fuller life through fantasy as well as fellowship. Only in the latter case do her future aspirations come within the scope of this book, although we cannot help being concerned with her present situation because the scattered houses she and her kind inhabit have so confused the development of the suburban communities which are our proper study.

We have said enough to distinguish between the true suburbia and the sporadic building of a suburban kind that threatens to engulf the countryside. It is the duty of the town planner to deal with the latter, and we can safely leave him to do so as long as we give him enough authority. Let him, if he finds such drastic measures necessary, compel all this residential building to remain within the limits of the town or within the boundaries of recognized suburban communities. But once he himself crosses those boundaries he must move with care, for he is operating in the kingdom of individualism itself. The technique of planning is all bound up with the application of scientific principles, and if such principles are laid down too rigidly they may interfere with the organic growth on which the suburban style depends. As we observed when speaking of visual taste in an earlier chapter, it will do no good to impose an advanced or academic idiom on people who are already evolving at their own slow pace a vernacular style based on very different standards, but suited to their own peculiar needs and aspirations, contemptible though this style may appear to the sophisticated. Similarly, the anarchy of the suburban jungle may appear contemptible to those with an urge towards the order and architectural rectitude brought about by scientific planning, but the town planner must deal tenderly with the slow unselfconscious process by which the suburban landscape grows. The suburban temperament, for example, as we have already noticed, values those fragments of the past which in the course of this process are continually being incorporated in the present. The inhabitant of suburbia is mildly interested in the planner's glimpses into an unfamiliar future but he will not welcome them with any enthusiasm until he is more confident that this future will bring him something of greater value than the tradition whose continuity it threatens to disturb.

There is plenty, of course, that the art of the town planner can contribute to improving the suburban environment, as long as he is content to play the part of guide rather than that of a didactic school-teacher. He can control the location of the suburb and set limits to its expansion, and ensure the proper provision of those services—educational, medical, recreational and the like—that will enable it to maintain the character of a self-contained community.

Another thing he can do is to control, in a general way, the actual quality of the building that goes on. Bad craftsmanship is a failing particularly prevalent in the suburbs, where rivalry among builders to produce the cheapest houses results in their being tempted to use cheap materials and mean dimensions and to rely on insufficiently skilled labour. In this the whole economic system under which building is conducted is at fault. The much maligned builder is, on the average, as honest a citizen as anyone else. He is only the instrument by means of which a competitive commercial system exploits the innocent consumer; the very system, incidentally, that has driven the suburban resident to take refuge in an environment in which he—for a change—is master, where he can build up at least the illusion that he is no longer a puppet of circumstances. Bad quality building has been aggravated by the growth of the hire-purchase system, which encourages the unscrupulous builder to make sure only that deterioration does not set in until the up-keep of the house has become the responsibility of the occupier. But jerrybuilding is no new thing. We read complaints of it as far back as the beginning of the last century. It is only now, when the personal pride of the craftsman has been largely lost, and we have not learnt to utilize instead the machine's reliability in reproducing a given standard of quality, that it has become a menace. However, all this is part of the much larger problem of how building methods can best adapt themselves to the advent of new materials and processes, a problem which, like that of the economics of house ownership, lies outside the scope of this book.

Compactness Above All

Getting back to the more local question of how town planning and similar legislation should be applied in the suburb, we can sum up our observations by saying that as things are at present (and as we have defined a suburb) a completely planned suburbia is almost a contradiction in terms. Scientific planning deals in the general, and in the operation of the law of cause and effect. The suburban style lays stress on the particular, and on the variety of the individual whim, which is itself reinforced by the never-ceasing ebb and flow of fashion in succeeding generations. But among particular efforts at legislation, the bye-laws which place a limit on the number of houses to the acre, though beloved by the garden-suburb sentimentalists, are the most fatal to the true suburban spirit. It is an essential part of its character that the suburb should constitute a world in itself, susceptible of delimitation. Above all things it needs to be compact. Space as such is not an asset, and a low density only dilutes the rich suburban landscape.

In our ideal suburb, and in the best and most mature of the older suburbs, villa and villa nestle cheek by jowl, and what space is left between them is occupied by a labyrinth of garage yards and tradesman's entrances, of potting sheds, conservatories and tool-houses, and the interstices are filled with a tangle of hedges and shrubberies. Each fence-enclosed garden, before and behind, is itself further subdivided by rose-grown pergolas and borders of sunflowers and hollyhocks. The view across each miniature lawn is interrupted by beds of dwarf conifers or towering pampas grass, and gravel paths wind in and out of the bushes.

We want no clearings in our jungle; only the small secluded lawns of the local bowling club, the open square of pavement planted with pollarded lime trees in front of the public library, the net-ball pitch adjoining the Girls' High School and the boys' asphalted playground screened by trees within its painted railing, carpeted now with flattened chestnut leaves. In the citadel of domesticity there is no call for crowds to assemble. Even on Armistice Day, when an open-air service is held in front of the memorial to the men who fell in the 1914 War, the congregation

87

must find places as best they can. The vicar, his surplice billowing in the blustering wind, stands just beneath the oaken lych-gate within which the names are inscribed, and facing him are the mayor and councillors and other notabilities, but the congregation flows away down the hill, round the corner half-way to the fire station, and straggles along the churchyard wall competing restlessly for points of vantage among the undulating landscape of gravemounds, interspersed with holly and elder, that constitutes the older portion of the burial ground.

Here is the original core round which the modern concretion called suburbia has gathered itself. There is also, of course, a new cemetery, bleakly specked with white marble. It lies outside the perimeter of the suburb proper, as do the school and club playing fields, their slender goal posts silhouetted against an unfamiliar expanse of sky. And nearby is an old deer park, now the public recreation ground, where perambulators are wheeled along asphalt paths and young mothers sit knitting and gossiping on sunny afternoons, sheltered from the wind by artificial grottoes with oyster shells set in their mossy walls. Suburbia can venture thus far out of its sheltering undergrowth, but its spirit is nourished among the winding roads where trees and gabled roof-peaks keep the expanse of sky within bounds, and especially in the treasured privacy of house and garden.

8

This Desirable Residence

As the amateur gardener admires the picture on the seedpacket, fully aware that the luxuriant growth depicted is a little larger and more highly coloured than life, yet half persuaded that something like it may indeed come true, so I would have the would-be pilgrim to suburbia regard the picture of an idyllic suburban environment given in some of the foregoing pages. It is not nearly so optimistic a picture as sceptics may assume if they have not taken the trouble to see for themselves, and the element of fantasy it contains is not something unreal with which I have chosen to invest it; at worst it is only an intensification of attributes that already exist wherever the suburban landscape has been allowed to flourish freely. It may be that the pilgrim will have to travel far and patiently before he comes on one suburban scene that combines all the charms I have described and is still free from the faults of which other critics have already made the world too conscious. Yet our enchanted jungle is far from being a myth.

Even if it were a myth, however, it would still represent the ideal to which the suburban temperament aspires. The very possession of such an ideal helps the suburban population towards a mood of creation, and one of the most necessary roles of the suburban environment is, as we have seen, to provide some opportunity of individual self-expression for people to whom it is otherwise denied. One moral of this book is that creative activity can only be encouraged among the mass of people by building on a foundation of their own existing modes of expression. For this purpose—especially when looking at the suburbs—sophisticated standards of taste and criticism can conveniently be forgotten. The method pursued under the guidance of such standards is to offer people 'good architecture' and hope that they will come to like it by habit. Now habits are all very well, but they are not a product of feeling, and the art of architecture requires the support of intense feeling. People can only learn to feel intensely by starting with the things that already mean something to them emotionally, and while the values on which the critics insist on basing their idea of architectural right and wrong remain aloof from the values by which people in the suburbs judge their own environment, they will have no feelings about architecture and it will get no share of their creative energy. A more useful method is to encourage people in their own creative efforts, entering emotionally into their lives to see where opportunities of this kind occur (watching sympathetically, for example, the conflict that goes on all the time between their fear of nonconformity and their urge to live fantastically) and recognizing creative achievement even when it outrages sophisticated taste.

It is possible that in due time the result of such encouragement might be to evoke 'good architecture' of its own accord. That sort of thing has happened in the past, but it will only happen in the modern suburb if outside conditions—especially economic conditions—permit the suburban ideal to coincide with the ideals of good taste cherished elsewhere. The architecture of the most civilised age in English history, the age of Queen Anne, has been described as a 'fusion of classic grace with vernacular energy' and the re-establishment in the suburbs of universal sophisticated standards of design would mean that a fusion of a similar kind had once more been achieved. It is possible that we are justified in looking towards such a future. But it is also possible that the suburbs ought to be looking towards a rather different future of their own. Various things have happened since Queen Anne died —notably the rise of commercialism discussed in another chapter— which make the picture more complicated now. Whether or not we care to identify classic grace with the intellectualism of the city, as an earlier passage in this book suggested we might do, and vernacular energy with regionalism, and say that a simple fusion of the two does not answer everybody's problem now that both are dominated by a new commercial world which neither classic grace nor vernacular energy will satisfy, there are still plenty of reasons for thinking that in the future some kind of hide-out for fantasy may always be needed, some province set apart for amateurishness and anarchy, such as the suburb at present provides.

That is one argument for respecting the fruits of suburban energy and feeling, even when we see them blossoming unbecomingly along arterial roads and along the cliff edges near coastal towns, and for not only respecting but admiring them when we see them filling the leafy valleys of Metroland with its own peculiar landscape, concealing a world the outside observer hardly knows. This world has a vitality which derives from its being a direct response to the demands of its own nature. The enemy of this vitality is not the vulgarity its critics generally associate with the suburb, but the genteel correctness of taste that tries to undermine it. Our attempt to interpret suburban ideals is an attempt to uncover the hidden springs of feeling in the apparently arbitrary and insensible.

There are, however, at least two dangers inherent in this approach. One is that in putting such a high value on people's instinctive aspirations as we have done when discussing what suburban people want of their environment, we may elevate mere instinct into something to be revered for its own sake. This was a fault of the Nazi philosophy, which worshipped instinct as a sort of super wisdom, superior to reason. But suburban aspirations, though inarticulate, are not mystical. They are susceptible of reasonable explanation. The fancy-dress means by which they are often achieved mislead us as to their nature. In the suburbs fantasy is functional

The other danger is a more obvious one: that by showing up the uselessness of imposing a sophisticated architectural idiom on people who are neither ready nor temperamentally willing to appreciate it, we appear to disparage the intrinsic worth of the particular idiom that this century is developing for its own purposes. That is to say, we appear to advocate clinging to tradition for its own sake, and find ourselves on the same side of the fence as the reactionaries and the people who dislike and discourage modern design for their own diverse reasons. The last thing I want to do is to depict the suburb as some phoney 'Merrie England' that has no part in the main stream of cultural development; in fact the more sympathy one has for the so-called 'modern movement' and the more trust in its future, the more one tends at the present moment to insist that it must keep in touch at all costs with the people it serves, and that the needs of suburban dwellers, as expressed in the architectural style they have evolved for themselves, is something it cannot afford to misunderstand. For this style, as I began by saying, is as well and ubiquitously rooted as any earlier vernacular.

The time has passed when the 'modern movement' had to be justified as an experiment. Its principles are now accepted, and it is part of the world a new generation is growing up with. The current problems are problems of procedure and of quality rather than of principle. We are particularly concerned with the preservation of human values and of continuity, since the very virtues of a machine aesthetic contain the germ of its destruction: the possibility that people—whether suburban individuals or metropolitan communities—may find it more and more difficult to contribute personally to the development of what should still be a humanistic art, however mechanized its technique.

One mistake, therefore, that modern architecture has to avoid making is the mistake of allowing itself to become a specialized art that can only be appreciated by the minority. For a minority art is a closed art, closed to the warming influence of popular enthusiasm and understanding. It also tends to be dogmatic and to lack the common touch that should enable it to reflect those human vagaries which are the foundation of architectural richness.

In the nineteenth century popular enthusiasm was concentrated on technical progress, and this gave even the most practical tasks the character of a mission to be fulfilled. The present century has become blasé about technical progress as a whole, though it still feels sufficiently strongly about things like motor cars and aeroplanes and radio sets. The twentieth-century equivalent of the tasks of mechanical invention that so uplifted the nineteenth is the problem of social adjustment to the mechanical world. The railway mania of the eighteen-forties is logically succeeded by the planning enthusiasm of the nineteen-forties, and the popular interest in nursery schools and welfare centres and underground car parks ought to be able to do for our society what, say, the laying of the Atlantic cable or the completion of the Thames Tunnel did for that of a hundred years ago; namely, bind people together with a sense of common purpose. The possession of this sense is what produces a truly vernacular character in architecture and design. We find it in the design of the suburban landscape, and there it can be developed still further as one aspect of modern architecture's growth towards maturity—not, it should be made quite clear, by the introduction of fancy-dress styles, but by fostering a modern aesthetic that allows romance and fantasy to flourish, as distinct from one dictated solely by rational scientific planning. Whether romance and fantasy are engaged in inspiring the creation of modern nursery schools or of traditional cottage homes, their part in the suburban set-up is a permanent one, even though at the present moment the common purpose of the suburbs may be primarily one of organizing a system of defences against the unkindness of a hostile world.

The suburban dweller must be excused for this preoccupation with establishing himself in his own private environment. For he has more and more to fight his personal battles in a world that always seems ready to burst into flames, in which the cataclysm seems only just round the corner. It is also a world that operates on a superhuman scale. No epidemic is worth speaking of unless its victims are numbered in millions; people are imprisoned by the thousand and starve by the hundred thousand. But the suburban dweller remains loyal to the significance of the individual, and his efforts are guided by this instinct. For him the problems that matter in the world are the problems within the scope of his own experience—hence the success of the kind of newspaper that caters specially for him, in which human stories are front-page news and world politics quite secondary. The real world to him is his suburb, where it is sufficient for him devotedly to cultivate his garden.

In order to be able to do so effectively he has evolved the environment described in this book, with its characteristic landscape style. That is how the suburb comes to be synthetic and self-contained. It cannot be repeated too often that it is not a modification of anything else; above all it is not a modification of the residential parts of towns. For towns have always grown up round some nucleus—a cathedral, a bridge over a river or a harbour—whereas the suburb has only grown up round itself. It is a world peculiar to itself and must be judged as such without prejudice.

Since the creator of suburban life is the individual, its essence lies in domesticity. As our pilgrim to suburbia says goodbye to the territory he has been so assiduously exploring, it is already beginning to get dark, and walking along the pavement he can see this essential domesticity—summarized, it may seem, for his benefit—in a series of peepshows, as he is privileged to look for a moment inside one front room after another, where the lights are already on but the curtains not yet drawn. He halts for a moment, perhaps, where family tea is taking place round a gate-leg table in the middle of the dining room. The table's well polished surface, already carpeted as it is by mats and runners of embroidered linen, is almost obscured by a multiplication of plates and cake-dishes and jugs, to say nothing of a large vase in the centre containing an arrangement of dried Cape gooseberries and gilded poppy pods. The family circle, beginning with the householder himself whose bald head has its back to the window, and ending with the youngest who waves his spoon petulantly in his high chair, is bathed in the amber light of the parchment-shaded floor standard in the corner, a light that is reflected from the oatmeal papered walls with their cut-out frieze of autumn-tinted foliage and from the fan-shaped mirror with cut and bevelled edges which hangs over the sideboard at the far end of the room.

This picture, occupying an illuminated rectangle in a darkening wall, is sharp but remote like a scene in a theatre. Our pilgrim moves on, for he is feeling a little guilty at finding himself enjoying a glimpse of a life that does not concern him; the actors are clearly only aware of each other, not of any audience that may be loitering beyond the ivied window-sill and the front garden below it, plunged in darkness like the orchestra pit. Yet there are several similar glimpses into the privacy of the home down this same street, for suburban dwellers, conscious of the rectitude of their lives and the superiority of their own brand of domesticity, are in no hurry to obscure it from chance observation. And elsewhere, where the curtains have already been drawn, the life that goes on behind is made evident by passing shadows and the glow of lights put on and off as members of the family move from room to room about their business.

But outside, by contrast, except for our solitary pilgrim all is deserted, for suburban life is not generally lived late out of doors. Only on long summer evenings does the suburban resident some-times sit on in the garden after darkness has set in, too contented to stir from the comfort of his deck chair on the lawn till he is driven in by the biting of midges and the chill of the dew striking up through the soles of his slippers. At other times the jungle keeps well under cover at night, and only the stirrings in the under-growth indicate the teeming life that inhabits it. The street is hushed so that the footsteps of a late visitor ring sharp and distinct, and so does the sing-song voice calling a dog in repeated summonses from the shadows of a barely visible porch. Nor can anything be seen to move, except when the headlamps of a car, passing the end of the road, throw a beam of ghostly light in quick succession over tree and hedge and porch and lamp-post, to die away on the edge of the pavement but to give, before it does so, brief glimpses of the variegated nature of the suburban landscape, that intricate mechanism, jewelled—as a watchmaker would say—in every movement.

The dog summoned from the shadowed porch, the cheerful tea table, the quiet between the passing car lights; there is the essence of the modern English domestic scene. For better or worse the English in this generation are becoming a nation of suburban dwellers, and the typical background of domestic life is now the winding road system of the suburban jungle, no longer the maze of city streets and slums where Dickens laid the scene of his stories nearly a century ago. For Dickens was the novelist of the urbanization of English life. He portrayed, in more than life-sized pictures, the fabulous quality and the violence and idiosyncrasy of teeming London. He showed romance and colour emerging even from metropolitan slums.

One day perhaps a Dickens of the suburbs will arise, to immortalize the life and language of suburbia. His task will be to portray individual character and idiosyncrasy similarly emerging from today's most typical setting; and also, like Dickens, to publicize abuses: the exploitation of the innocent suburban householder by Building Societies and speculative builders, and the loneliness of the housewife marooned at the end of the newest road in the spreadeagled building estate. But, as Dickens proves so well, only someone who first discovers for himself, through his own affection for it, the peculiar virtues of the world in which he is interested, can fairly isolate its vices.

This world of the suburbs should be entered and explored with due respect and decorum. When the trouble has been taken to uncover some of the romance that lurks behind its shrubberies and to record the sentiments on which the suburban spirit is nourished, then these elusive territories—now the heart of England—past which we unobservantly speed in motor cars and trains and over whose roof-dappled greenery we may all soon be cruising in aeroplanes, will no longer be a strange unknown country.